Working from Home
for a Harmonious Life

Luc Desroches

Pottersfield Press
Lawrencetown Beach, Nova Scotia, Canada

Library and Archives Canada Cataloguing in Publication

Title: Working from home for a harmonious life / by Luc Desroches.
Names: Desroches, Luc, author.
Identifiers: Canadiana (print) 2020027824X | Canadiana (ebook) 20200278258 | ISBN 9781989725313 (softcover) | ISBN 9781989725320 (EPUB)
Subjects: LCSH: Telecommuting. | LCSH: Telecommuting—Psychological aspects. | LCSH: Flexible work arrangements. | LCSH: Flexible work arrangements—Psychological aspects.
Classification: LCC HD2336.3 .D47 2020 | DDC 331.25/68—dc23

Cover design: Gail LeBlanc

Pottersfield Press gratefully acknowledges the financial support of the Government of Canada for our publishing activities. We also acknowledge the support of the Canada Council for the Arts and the Province of Nova Scotia which has assisted us to develop and promote our creative industries for the benefit of all Nova Scotians.

Pottersfield Press
248 Leslie Road
East Lawrencetown, Nova Scotia, Canada, B2Z 1T4
Website: www.PottersfieldPress.com
To order, phone 1-800-NIMBUS9 (1-800-646-2879) www.nimbus.ns.ca

Printed in Canada   FOREST STEWARDSHIP FSC COUNCIL

Pottersfield Press is committed to protecting our natural environment. As part of our efforts, this book is made of material from well-managed FSC®-certified forests and other controlled sources.

Opinions expressed are solely my own and do not express the views or opinions of my employer.

Dedication

To my wife for all your love and support in living a harmonious life. This book would not exist without our daily conversations and your amazing tolerance for my very early morning and evening writings, and for doing more than your share in maintaining the hundreds of tasks with our three young daughters and a Labrador retriever.

Contents

Author's Note

This book was mostly written pre-COVID-19, when working from home was more the exception than the rule. But with almost every employee on the planet being encouraged to work from home where possible, COVID-19 has dramatically changed everything and millions have been forced to adapt, forced to leave the safety of the known. An explosion of resources has emerged, including technological, emotional, and psychological resources.

Before COVID-19, the experience felt more like a solo one, a lone wolf going against the current of the typical commuting-worker environment. Teleworking due to COVID-19 is more a mass social experiment with experts in every field helping the transition.

Although most will likely return to their previous workplaces, I suspect a great many who have tasted the nectar will want to continue to telework. For those who enjoy their work most of the time, have increased their productivity, and feel more balanced, this is a major opportunity for significant costs to be saved by both the employee and employer, and for all to have a more harmonious and better life.

After this pandemic crisis, working from home will be an easier transition. The resources are now in place, the direct knowledge of how to make it happen exists, and the experience is no longer so unfamiliar. COVID-19 has left its traumatizing mark on the world, but the ability now for so many to work from home is a positive element, for both humanity and all our relations on this beautiful, interconnected planet.

Introduction

I began working in cubicle environments in 2003, and for a while I enjoyed the experience, both personally and professionally. I adapted well to each job, and always received praise at my performance reviews, with positive comments on not just my overall performance, but on teamwork, supervision, and other social competencies. You could say that, in many ways, I excelled in this environment. However, as years passed, I came to better understand what called me in life, and having more deeply discovered my true sense of autonomy, things gradually changed.

Until one day in my office cubicle I surprised myself by saying, out loud, "Maybe I could just stay home ..."

It came from a profound place in me, like a gut feeling, which also scared me – it felt counterintuitive; it wasn't what I thought I'd wanted for many years. A colleague looked at me and said, "Don't say that," which was comforting; it kept me in the safe harbours of what I knew – that my colleagues cared, I mattered to the team, and that the social cohesion at work was worth all the inconveniences. Still, I could not ignore what my gut was telling me. There I was at my standing desk, looking around the cubicle environment and feeling sad, acutely aware of all the "inconveniences," like the office psychological attacks and toxicity, both human and environmental.

Now, I honestly believe nobody is truly toxic or bad, but the cubicle environment can bring out the worst in people and may particularly affect the driven, those who are so focused on their tasks that they may be seen as "too intense" and unsocial. So, in 2016, with my own calling already surfacing, an unexpected offer for a three-year assignment came my way.

I was ready to make the jump, and my working from home journey began.

The assignment was a promotion closely related to what I had been doing since 2007, which was building and maintaining positive relationships with Indigenous communities as a federal public servant. It was part of a proposed $15 billion project, the most significant of its kind in Canada, and I would report directly to Ottawa, thousands of kilometres from my home city of Dieppe, New Brunswick.

My past experience was highly sought and directly relevant to the assignment: the newly created team needed someone who had built strong relationships with the potentially affected communities, and I lived in proximity to these same communities. When my new supervisor offered to set up a remote office in my hometown, I immediately proposed working from my residence. It would save the employer money, I pointed out, plus save time by eliminating the commute (thus increasing my performance). We agreed to try it out for a few months.

It didn't take me long to realize the holy grail I had stumbled upon.

Looking back nearly four years later, I see how ready I was for a change, to create a new beginning. The pain of the cubicle environment was far greater than the fear of working from home. To find a bigger, better adventure, I had to leave behind what I'd known so far, and I did so in one great leap, not just a few days here and there.

It was 100 percent full immersion, but in just a few weeks I formed productive habits and have never wanted to return to a cubicle. Being a father of three young daughters with a full-time, demanding job, this set-up, with its additional time and energy, made other personal passions and muses possible.

Such as writing this book.

This book is intended to be a call to action by describing my own working-from-home experience, other people's experiences, and the latest in science and research. I will describe the profound contrast of my years of working in a cubicle to working in the comfort of my home office and how I improved my performance, focus, health, well-being, and happiness, leading to an overall much better experience of day-to-day living.

Although this is not a book about spirituality (or religion), my spiritual realizations and experiences have been the most important elements to harmoniously navigating working from home, and, in fact, life in general. Throughout this book, I make reference to words that point to this deeper realm, such as awareness, source, being, grounding, energy, and frequency. I believe this deeper aspect of life is intimately linked to all we do and we all have different ways to experience or name it. Some call it God, a higher realm, Buddha nature, or Ananda. The list is long. Personally, the teachings of Adyashanti, Eckhart Tolle, Alan Watts, and Wayne Dyer (to name just a few) have helped me tremendously over the years.

I am grateful to have been enlightened by so many beautiful souls.

Working From Home Gives You ...

A better life with better lived values

There are numerous advantages for working remotely, advantages which millions of people enjoy around the world every day. This book, through my research and my personal experiences, explores the advantages and the drawbacks of working remotely, all with the goal of helping you decide whether working from home is right for you.

I have been a teleworker since 2016, and by diving into my own journey and psyche, I hope my words will resonate with you, showing how working from home can allow you to be a better human being by bringing better life experiences and helping to implement the following values more deeply and more evenly:

- Creativity
- Curiosity
- Judgment (critical thinking)
- Love of learning
- Bravery
- Honesty

- Perseverance
- Zest (enthusiasm, lust for life)
- Kindness
- Love
- Social Intelligence
- Perspective (Big Picture, Street Smarts)
- Being Fair (equitable)
- Leadership
- Prudence (thinking things through)
- Teamwork
- Forgiveness
- Humility
- Self-regulation (discipline, self-control)
- Appreciation of Beauty and Excellence
- Gratefulness
- Hope
- Humour
- Spirituality[1].

Author Alexis Rockley explains in her book *Find Your F*ckyeah*[2] that many people place too much effort on just a few of these values, instead of having a more balanced attention to all. If working remotely helps you balance these aspects of your life (i.e. by swapping gridlock traffic for sipping your tea while contemplating in your comfortable rocking chair), then it is a very good sign that this is the right decision for you. Later in this book (see Figure 2 on page 90), I show how Indigenous values and knowledge weave beautifully with these 24 aspects.

Better lived values means a better life.

Increased productivity and focus

Great creative minds think like artists but live like accountants.

– David Brooks, New York Times

A two-year study[3] by Stanford University found that there was an impressive increase in work productivity among people who worked from home. The study of 500 people who worked both remotely and in a traditional setting concluded that the productivity among home-based workers was equal to an extra day's work each week.[4]

Typical workplaces don't allow for much "inner work" – observing yourself internally as opposed to looking externally to your own body and life – mostly because we are around other people and tend to be too distracted. It is hard to discern a source of un-comfortability when there's a barrage of people distracting each other. Is fading/poor attention an unconscious way of trying to find comfort, one that could be better found in our own space, one that is forgotten, like noticing we are breathing? At home, I can more easily concentrate, rejuvenate, and therefore be better prepared for the next uncomfortable deadline or task, *and* have extra energy to spend time with my wife or attend my daughter's evening sports activity.

The TV series *The Office* is popular for a reason: people relate. It's entertaining drama on TV, but unfortunately depicts the often concealed and devastating toxicity of workplaces. Of course there is no TV show about working from home – it would be too boring – but this "boring" is the perfect non-distracting environment you may need for your best life.

Improved health in all dimensions (i.e. mental, emotional, physical, spiritual)

We spend most of our time at work, so why not make being present at work more attainable? By "being present," I refer to being what some people call grounded. The work itself may be stressful at times, and pull us out of presence, but this is more easily intermingled with presence in a grounded environment, such as the one carved at home. I am healthier and wealthier by having not just my own quiet space, but more time for journalling, more quality time with my loved ones, and, during breaks, more energy and more adventures (more on that later). During the day I have more natural dopamine in my system, less cortisol-inducing stress, and much more presence.

From this place I can make a more positive impact.

The workplace is also where we spend most of our waking time. Therefore, improving this critical environment improves every other part of our lives. If bringing peace, joy, and presence to the world is a high value for you, or if you want to have presence more often while also doing meaningful work (that you hopefully love most of the time) and get paid well, then it makes sense to set yourself up in the best work environment as possible.

Later in the book I describe my work with Indigenous communities in Canada, and discuss Indigenous values, approaches to well-being, and the medicine wheel to describe how working from home, aligned with important values, can bring a better equilibrium.

Better relationships and social connection

Working from home, provided you have a peaceful environment, gives you the neutral space you need to find your own melody, which is often found in the stillness of your own company. We may say we have friends at our workplace, but we often don't look deeply enough. More commonly we have more superficial interactions and the artificial perception that some human beings are above or below others, often physically demonstrated with big corner offices versus small windowless cubicles.

Since leaving a workplace of hundreds, I have maintained contact with only a few, but have greatly increased the quality time with my closest relationships. For example, I usually pick Fridays to invite a friend, perhaps even a former colleague, to meet during lunchtime, which helps replenish my desire for quality social interaction. In other words, I have more quality interactions versus superficial quantity.

During a presentation that my wife and I attended, Brigitte Racine, a well-respected authority on child behaviour,[5] discussed the importance of quality time between parents and their children, and recommended an optimal quality-time period of 20 minutes of one-on-one uninterrupted play. In the barrage of activities, many families with more than one child find it difficult to squeeze in these 20 minutes, but it is well worth it and is much appreciated by my three young daughters. This practice makes me and my wife realize that it is not enough to be physically in the same house or same cubicle space, but that there needs to be an intentional effort to better meet our social desires, even if just for a few minutes at a time.

Since working from home, I have found more time for these golden moments, like when I trade my morning commute time for a game with my oldest daughter before she leaves for school. These are also the rare times where I can ask the hard questions all parents should ask their teens.

There's a beautiful sweetness in connecting with kindred spirits. Life is better when shared, but be careful not to overshare, where you lose touch with your own beauty/energy. Like a mighty whale that needs to come up for air, you inhale the sweetness of your own alone time before you submerge and give the best of yourself to others, whether a 20-minute kid's game, a meal with a loved one, or a phone conversation with a colleague from the comfort of your home.

Working From Home: Is It Right For You?

To know if working from home is a good fit, there are many factors to consider. The following checklist highlights some of the important fundamentals, all of which increase the odds that telecommuting is right for you:

✓ You enjoy your time alone, where you often get energized and rejuvenated;

✓ You understand how it feels to "be alone, and not be lonely";

✓ Your work can be done from home and meets the Ikigai test (see page 90) – essentially doing something you enjoy most of the time, is meaningful for you, valuable to society, and pays adequately;

✓ You have already experienced the typical office workspace with colleagues and have come to intimately understand office dynamics, and you were able to perform well;

✓ You have a healthy dose of emotional and social intelligence[6] which helps increase your resilience and performance;

✓ You have a suitable home or remote[7] designated area that allows you to be organized, ergonomically comfortable, and gives you quiet space;

✓ You have enough discipline and are willing to implement certain ground rules[8] such as limited distractions, clear work hours and breaks;

✓ You have SMART (Specific, Measurable, Attainable, Results oriented, and Timebound) performance objectives;

✓ You have a supportive supervisor who allows regular bilateral check-ins to talk about work and personal matters, which increases psychological safety[9];

✓ You are able to plan your own social connections (quality time with family and friends).

Pros and cons of working from home: personal experience

Obviously, if working from home has many more advantages than drawbacks for you, that's a good sign. To explain why working from home is best for me, it's helpful to mention both the advantages and how I manage the drawbacks. Here's a quick summary of some of the advantages:

• No more daily traffic, and no more needing to leave before rush hour;

• Stress levels at optimum for best performance and creative passions;

- Able to take on lots of work, work more effectively and efficiently with mind-energy to spare at the end of the day;

- Fewer decisions to make (e.g. what to wear, where to park, remembering your lunch bag), which increases capacity to make better decisions;

- Can take better mid-day breaks,[10] step outside, ground yourself, and fill your soul in one deep breath;

- Can use your days fully, less wasted time;

- Have much more time and energy outside your "official work hours";

- Able to escape the office's social dynamics, the distraction of unnecessary meetings or social gatherings and unscheduled chats at the water cooler[11];

- Have more control over your social encounters and see more people you want to see, like friends, family, and neighbours;

- Easier to avoid virus propagation (e.g, the flu, coronavirus), or allergens such as perfumes and dust;

- Can spend more time with your calming pet;

- Have more silence and quiet space for the mind;

- Is better on the family emotional equilibrium;

- Can enjoy your home space where you spend the most money (mortgage/rent and related home bills);

- Can listen to music, and if you feel the need, sing or scream out loud.

Conversely, here are the most common drawbacks (note that these can be significantly minimized in most cases – there are tips and best practices described in this book):

- Isolation: feelings of heavy heart, loneliness, sadness, left outside of team, abandoned or disconnected;
- Fear of Missing Out (FOMO): the fear that you'll wake up one day feeling like you missed out on too many social interactions or activities;
- Unclear or unhealthy boundaries: feeling like everything is jumbled together, no clear distinction between work and personal life;
- Overindulging in distractions;
- Bad eating habits.

There are various methods to lessen the drawbacks, such as remembering to notice the darker feelings of isolation as opposed to trying to drown them out with more distractions. Remembering the much longer list of advantages and feeling grateful (a very simple practice, although not always easy to do) can help establish equilibrium and resilience.

With COVID-19 forcing many into teleworking, there's been a rapid acceleration of tools allowing better online communications and more flexible work arrangements (which accommodate family or other obligations). Most importantly, there's been significant social and cultural acceptance of teleworking and many teammates and supervisors now better understand the realities and therefore are better able to offer technical and even psychological support.

Note: There are online quizzes which give another indication if working from home is for you. I have included two of these in the Recommended Resources section at the end of this book.

My Story

The object of life is not to be on the side of the majority, but to escape finding oneself in the ranks of the insane.

– Marcus Aurelius

In July 2016, I dove head first into a challenging new job that not only did I love, but that, except for occasional travel, I could do without leaving home. Four years later it continues to be a deepening journey, one that's superbly aligned with a fulfilling life. My happiness and life experiences have improved, in depth and in breadth, by increasing my time and focus on better values.

Having spent over a dozen years in a typical office environment, I feel well-placed to write about the pros and cons of both work situations. While some of the work-from-home advantages are obvious (the convenience, the peacefulness), I want to write about the inner perspective, and why I can more easily accept the challenges of my job, remain enthusiastic about my work, and perform better.

Office buildings quickly feel like a kind of prison for me, and I work best in my own space. Working from home allows me to spend more uninterrupted time where I want to spend it, and because of that I am less frazzled at the end of the day.

Like painfully exercising for 30 minutes at a gym to enjoy healthier days afterwards, working from home is best enjoyed as a result of the fruits of hard labour, those earned experiences that are piled high in the background, such as life-affirming values and an understanding of team dynamics. For me, values such as self-discipline, courage, perseverance (grit), and teamwork were formed in various sports and when in the trenches of the workplace. These experiences must be found in more conventional environments (schools, office buildings) before they can be reflected in remote work. It helps to know the difference between having the occasional frazzled day at home, which sometimes happens if I skip my mid-day break, compared to being frazzled every day at my past workplaces regardless of the breaks I would take.

By sharing my experience, I hope to help change the conversation, present a more positive view of tele-working for the long term. Like Morpheus in *The Matrix*, I am telling you a truth you may not have considered, one that could significantly change your life. (You could say that COVID-19 has been "Morpheus" for millions of people by forcing teleworking almost overnight.) I see news articles emphasizing the negative aspects of working from home, such as a lack of social interaction and mental health issues, without mentioning the advantages, things that often tip the scale significantly.

It's important to realize that the technology which allows teleworking (for me and many other "knowledge workers"[12]) is the same exponentially growing technology (i.e., Artificial Intelligence) that will continue to disrupt the job market and will require workers to be much more versatile. The combination of technology and teleworking creates a fertile ground for more presence, creativity, peace, and for bringing inner knowledge to the outer world. Minimal tools are required; attention and self-discipline are often the best currency we can give to ourselves and to the world.

Until I jumped, I had no way of knowing that working from home was for me. And it was very much an inward jump. I followed the subtle, still voice that was softly nudging me, embracing me, saying, "All is well, you are enough, just be." I had to trust that I could work and be home. Many humans were doing it, and more and more are going to do it. It makes financial, environmental, spiritual, mental, physical, and emotional sense.

Working from home is a fierce journey that is lived internally and noticed by few. It doesn't scream to the world the way big offices and three-piece suits do. It has allowed me to focus more on my work and to grow as a person.

Quiet is the new loud

I shout peace and contentment in a world where most people are much too addicted to *doing* and to digital distractions. Leaving the office building can be like weaning off several addictions at once, although any withdrawal symptoms may not be visible. I am lucky to say that I love the work I do. *Ikigai* is a Japanese term for "a reason for being" or finding your life purpose and I am lucky to say that I seemed to have found my Ikigai, and I think we can all find our Ikigai even though it may change often in a lifetime. By having lived a variety of experiences and jobs, I have felt the contrast of veering off the path before returning to my Ikigai.

Variety? I had a job at Dairy Queen where I would be regularly burned by cooking oils, then was liberated into a summer of lifeguarding, and later, a rescue specialist with the Canadian Coast Guard. I spent four years in university studying kinesiology and then three years in law school, after which I returned to the federal government where I have held several positions since 2004.

I now play on the edges, working from home, having diplomatic relations with other nations within my own beautiful country. I'm at the cutting edge of what I do, beyond the political and media streams. I'm in my prime years to contribute and serve both professionally and in my personal muses, such as writing this book. I play in the abstract in service to humanity. I'm at the creative edges, enjoying the ride while it lasts.

Working from home was more life calling me than my deliberate planning. It was an unexpected offer, and the well-timed pull was immense. My office environment had gotten more and more difficult over the years, and this unknown path was a liberation for my growing soul, one that prefers being outdoors and free in my own space. It can almost all happen seamlessly on its own – the pull is so great, you have trouble going in any other direction when your path is calling you.

Working from home is a way of life. It permeates you, if you allow it. It's a recovery, renewal, a connection to both blissful and heavy emotions, an adjustment for the better; it's closer to the heart, closer to the truth.

Since 2008, I have spent more and more time during the day in an introspective "place"; it has changed my life, often in unforeseen ways, and continues to do so. It's the accumulation of subtle changes of direction, and decisions and intentions made along the path. The path has led me to being 100 percent at home for work, and I ran straight through my fears. (Prior to COVID-19, I felt like a lone wolf but now, with so many doing the same, there's been an explosion of additional support.)

I now have more leisure time. I do not get "bored" like when I was a kid. There are endless activities, like walking with my wife, tennis with my daughters, Frisbee at the beach, lunching with a friend, disc golf, park strolls, runs, movies, reading, swimming, and planning the next family vacation trip. I have, in a normal work-week, some 70 hours of potential leisure time when I remove the 37.5 hours of work and 49 hours of sleep.

Much of that time is spent bringing kids to activities or doing household tasks, but there is still much pure leisure time.

I have a full bookshelf and piles here and there of books. I have been enthusiastically reading for self-improvement since 2004 and have taken all kinds of journeys, mostly inner. I remember reading Einstein's biography, contemplating the theory of relativity while on a bus to my workplace in Halifax, Nova Scotia. I remember Robin Sharma's *The Monk Who Sold His Ferrari* and injecting its potent knowledge into countless conversations.

I still practise Sharma's habits, like waking early, something I was lucky to talk to him about in person in 2005. It's simple, but it's a game changer. Without those early hours in my life, you would not be reading this book. Meditation and physical activity were also vital, which are described in *The 5 AM Club*, his latest book. I have hundreds of books with all kinds of tips in all kinds of areas. I particularly enjoy the ones that make me stop and savour that moment of realization.

As Robin Sharma says, "Your life is worth recording." I have more time to record not just my insights, but my life in general. It brings out my creative juices. In the same way the recordings and books of other authors have helped me, perhaps my book will nudge you to take time to pause, reflect, and come to deeper realizations. Like an inspiring quote on a Friday, it can be a 10-second pause within the fray of the workday.

Just one idea can change your life.

If my working-from-home story resonates with you, then you're probably open to an awakening. Old structures are sometimes best left aside so new creative endeavours can flourish.

For as long as I can remember, I've wanted things like more money, fast cars and motorbikes, a cottage, a boat, and travel. Like many North Americans, I am part of the top 1 percent of humans on this planet in terms of money and materials (more than $32,400 US in annual income)[13], but I still have this insatiable "wanting and grasping" feeling, a feeling that would still exist even if I were a multi-millionaire. It has a close cousin of feeling inadequate, like "I'm not enough."

It's a time where I don't truly see what's around me. My ego tends to reside in mostly unfounded financial concerns and attaches itself to the pursuit of a thousand things, distorting the fact that *this moment is enough*, that *all is well now*. These are also the type of mental constraints that could have prevented me from working from home. Why? Because I equated the big offices with more pay, better connections, more lust for things, and a better lifestyle.

That was before I learned that bliss can be found in a simpler environment.

There is only now. Working from home, I am physically closer to my relations, to my kids, family, and dog. I am closer to my inner peace and quiet bliss, and closer to seeing the cosmic play of Samsāra[14], content with *being* before doing and doing with more being.

Some say, "Lucky you, you got it made"; lots say, "Oh, how do you like it?" or "I couldn't do it." Most people I speak with inquire about the social aspect, being alone most of the time and the lack of human contact, and the ensuing sadness or undisciplined loafing they imagine it to be. However, I believe that people underestimate the power of being alone much too quickly.

Since 2016, many of my conversations have involved the subject of working from home and I've informally interviewed others who were either working from home or questioning whether it would be right for them. I've helped hire high-performing colleagues who are currently thriving at home and also helped others decide it was not for them. I've seen friends and neighbours flourish and others struggle and look to return to the office building environment.

What I have found that has helped me and others most in these conversations was to talk about the deeper psychological aspects, mentioning both the benefits and challenges and how, most often, the pros overwhelmingly outweigh the cons. We talk about the importance of the regular check-in calls to maintain healthy social connections, or the higher performance we deliver. We talk about our personality types and all the things we don't miss from our past work experiences. We also talk about how we make it work with our families, managers, colleagues, and friends.

For those of us who have been at it for a longer period of time, we can quickly go beyond superficial small talk and connect more from the heart, emotions, and soul after only a few probing questions. We connect like any people who share an interest or passion that fulfills them at a deep level.

You could view working from home as a great re-arrangement, a change in our thinking that can greatly improve mental health for the more introverted worker, or the driven, high-performing ambivert. According to some research, nearly half of all American citizens lean towards "introverted" on the personality spectrum,[15] so working from home may be better for many. If you're curious to learn more about ambiverts and whether you may be one, you can Google various tests, including Travis Bradberry's "9 signs that you're an ambivert" – online at Forbes.com. According to Bradberry, "Personality traits exist along a continuum and the vast majority of us aren't introverts or extroverts – we fall somewhere in the middle."

I'm a driven ambivert. When I bought Douglas Brackmann's book *Driven*[16], I was hoping to gain more insight into other loved ones' attention deficit and hyperactivity disorder (ADHD), but I found, to my surprise, that I am one of the people with "Drive" as described in the book. Although I would not be diagnosed with ADHD, my mind has some ADHD patterns which may make it easier for me to succumb to distraction.

Dr. Brackmann explains that some 10 percent of the population "are born with a drive" and it is a powerful tool when the driven realize that although they will constantly strive to improve everything in an often obsessive manner, they are also okay right now. Dr. Brackmann describes specific meditations for the driven, and approaches to find balance and awareness that help us embrace our inner drives in a healthier manner. Working from home, in fact, is ideal for many people with ADHD or who are "driven," as they are more prone to be distracted in a typical office cubicle and can maintain their focus much easier in a quieter environment.

As with many socially aware and competent people, I'm easily able to have conversations on a variety of subjects. I'm not particularly quiet or easygoing, although I may appear very calm. I tend to overanalyze and can be easily overwhelmed, worrying about past actions (sometimes months or years ago), until they're brought to awareness and all worry vanishes. Awareness encompasses both joy and strife. Awareness is elusive, yet so importantly enlightening. My quarrelsome psyche is what makes the contrast even more obvious when I re-ground myself, and I don't know of a better way to re-ground on a consistent daily basis than the joy of working in my own home.

Such is the plight of many ambiverts, able to function well and pick up the energy of a room, but often highly drained afterwards. My personality is put to good use at work during diplomatic meetings, maintaining good relations, and advancing complex matters using my creative side. I tend to flesh out truth and creativity, which go hand in hand. I bring analytical structure and agendas into discussions, but still keep the flow going. Sometimes silence is the best way to get the truth. When a group of people are in flow, there's no time for too much mind. The quiet of home makes me better prepared for these meetings, tapping into flow/intuition to better plan what can happen.

My senses may be overwhelmed, perhaps quicker than most. I suspect this hypersensitivity is prevalent for the introverted or ambivert types, the same types who are often well-suited for a more peaceful and quiet environment. Hypersensitivity can be like a superpower in certain environments, such as gauging the energy of an important meeting and connecting at a more intuitive level with people's emotions and deeper intentions beyond the spoken words. In a typical loud office workplace, this same hypersensitivity made me feel much more "frazzled" at the end of the day because of the cumulative draining activities (i.e. the multitude of distractions in open offices) and insufficient calming breaks.

Working from home counters the negative effects and helps me recuperate much quicker. At home, my energy rarely enters over-stress levels (i.e., anxiety, meltdown) and additionally, I have, as previously mentioned, more available stress releases.

I have an amazing artist oasis in my own backyard, where I love basking in the summer sun during my lunch break. I nourish my creative self by waking early, reading thoughtful books, and watching inspiring videos. (And implementing the teachings that resonate most.) Through exercising, meditating, going on vacations, and surrounding myself with what I love, my life is good. I rarely deal with toxic people or environments. I avoid overindulging in alcohol, cannabis (legal in Canada), TV, work, sex, or food. I can better maintain or improve my physical condition by having more time for activities such as lifting weights or relaxing in a sauna. I can better appreciate my immediate family, who nurture me as much as I do them.

I have date nights, and artist dates; the latter are activities to help discover and recover our creative selves, as described in Julia Cameron's book *The Artist's Way*. For me artist dates include movies, plus softball, ball hockey, golf, running, swimming, weight lifting, canoeing the Restigouche river, kayaking, hunting, fishing, walking my dog in a park, or resting in a hammock. There's random ice cream excursions, and riding my bike at lunch. I could even go skydiving if I choose ... The point is, with the lowered stress and the additional free time, I can better experience life, and do all these activities that call me.

The moment my wife and kids walk out in the morning, peaceful silence is in the house. Me and my space, my time, nobody watching over me, no social mask, just being. I replace the morning commute with music, comedy, writing, or reading books, then start work that I am paid for at 8:30 a.m. Although I sometimes change my work hours around my busy family life, I primarily maintain my work hours from 8:30 a.m. to 4:30 p.m., as this aligns with my work colleagues' hours and when my house is quiet.

At home, you can dress in your comfortable T-shirt and jeans, not the usual long-sleeve business shirts with neutral colours that muffle creativity. Not only are you comfortable in your own skin, but you're wearing your preferred clothes. Not only is your mood more peaceful, but you can listen to music that aligns with your mood. Alone but not lonely, I bask in my calm environment and contribute even more to society with all the beautiful undistracted creative time.

I sometimes fall back to a subtle worry, back to a sort of suffering ... then I see it, and immediately it's not so heavy. I sometimes hold on to past "issues" for much longer than is practically useful, and I can become aware of that also. It feels good to find perspective, like when a good friend says, "Let it go, man, no need to worry about that!" Being able to "let go" of attachments is one of the key ways to re-ground yourself when working from home, because this can be done on your own. In fact, I find it easier to "let go" in my own authentic space where I'm not distracted or spiralling farther with other people's attachments and moods. As a bonus, when I do connect with others, I'm much more pleasant and able to help make lives better for everyone.

Doing what I love matters, much more than whether it's at home or in an office or outdoors. Combining working from home and doing what I love or what calls me most is a powerful combination. Some travels away are great for my adventure wealth/health, and some weekly Friday lunches out are good for the soul.

I have deeply enjoyed journalling and writing about working from home. Journalling is a key piece to staying grounded, and I try to do it every morning. It removes the psychic webs, improves my workdays, and reminds me how wonderful it is to have my own space to reflect. It is a beautiful act of liberation and kindness for my soul. There is nothing like living the experience and then writing about it. Journalling purifies the mind and brings more purpose to your life and appreciation of what you have.

A bit like Marcus Aurelius' *Meditations*, my writing

often takes the form of daily reflections about what I'm currently doing. As well described in the book *The Artist's Way*, doing three pages every morning elevates your life and awakens your creativity. This practice alone, done while most people are still sleeping, has allowed me to write this book and start my days filled with gratefulness, exercise, meditation, and deep work. Writing about this roller coaster of a life helps immensely.

Journalling helps to find peace and it allows space for all my interpretations, space for gratitude; the good oozes out once I notice the mental chatter. Like finding a billion-dollar bill in your pocket before going to work "for a living"... it's already there, hidden under the chatter. Journalling is like a pilot glancing at his flight instruments even if, to the naked eye, there has been no obvious course deviation.

I highly recommend journalling in the morning, and that you journal about anything, including the experience of working from home. Similar to meditation, journalling focuses my mind and is one of the best ways I know to improve all facets of health. And because it can be done alone, it is such a powerful tool for people working from home. It is the best way to start my day, and I usually journal between 5 a.m. and 7 a.m.

Journalling can become a passion in itself. It's a productive meditation and helps to untangle psychic webs by bringing together the mental, the spiritual, the emotional, and the physical. The mental, or mind aspect, includes thoughts; spiritual, the act of openness to writing; emotional, the focused awareness of "now"; and physical, the actual act of writing, of pen and paper coming together. Work often has much more mind involved. This practice brings the whole "wheel" into play.

I remember journalling during breaks back when I worked in an office building; even there it would cleanse the soul. This method and approach forces you to sit down and listen to what is flowing through. You are, at that moment, connected to your purpose.

Life is worth contemplating daily.

Working from home is soaking in what I already have in a fuller way. No need to look further. I can bring my laptop or book outside with the sun in my face or to my favourite corner in the house. My heart and soul thank me for this. My productivity has increased in this environment.

Bringing my kids to daycare is too often a big pull at the heart. Working from home reduces that pull by having a shorter commute, and I can pick them up earlier or spend more quality time with them before school. I appreciate their presence so much more now and can now offer them a "real" summer, with time at their own house with a teen, a kind of older sister, to supervise them. They can spend their summer doing all kinds of outdoor activities (like bicycling everywhere, or swimming in the pool), playing to their hearts' content with less restraints. As a bonus, I can catch glimpses of them during the day. With moms now working outside of home, a dad working from home can have a great, positive impact.

Working from home is a call from the heart and soul and a call to be more grounded, present, and likely to function much better, cleaner, smoother with a calm, soothing flow of creative energy, a counterforce against our often much-too-distracted families with big and small screens.

Working from home brings major relief from the tyranny of workplace "groupthink" and unnecessary office politics. A good analogy to this is the bystander effect, which is defined by *Psychology Today* as occurring when "the presence of others discourages an individual from intervening in an emergency situation. The greater the number of bystanders, the less likely it is for any one of them to provide help to a person in distress. People are more likely to take action in a crisis when there are few or no other witnesses present."[17]

The type of work I've done, and that many do, requires individual team members to carry out their work in their own uninterrupted space with only occasional check-ins and collaborations with the group (no more than one or two hours per day). The "tyranny" I mention was being physically pulled into too many meetings for far too long. The physical distance created between colleagues by working from home forces people to think twice, do more advanced planning, and pick the right people as opposed to being dragged into open-space cubicle meetings just because you happen to be in the vicinity (and distracting other cubicle colleagues). Since working from home, these gatherings have therefore become much more focused and strategic with fewer participants, as well as clearer time blocks and items to discuss.

Having experienced more time alone, I notice that

now I react differently in social settings. While I wait for a friend or colleagues at a restaurant, I feel content in my own skin. As colleagues or teammates surround me, it may feel awkward but okay, just a mash of different energies and personalities. Trying to satisfy others is not a place to fill a void, and I tend to not appreciate the food I'm eating when I'm with co-workers because I'm too busy thinking, listening, and talking.

It's good to notice how it all plays out, even if I may prefer to leave and get back home, be in my comfortable shorts, barefoot and working in peace. I don't need to socialize to be content, at least not in this manner and certainly not every day. I mostly attribute my expanded comfort in my alone time with the spiritual teachings I've practised (like walking meditations) and the fact that I've been able to practise more often.

It matters to know myself better. This knowledge is powerful, especially when I see it at play in real time. With this knowledge, I am more comfortable in my discomforts. It's okay to sit alone with less fanfare. And it's okay to socialize even if it secretly feels awkward. And it's okay that I prefer to have deep conversations with few, rather than loud conversations with many. I no longer feel shame for not always being "the extrovert" or physically with a group, like when I would walk alone in a high school hallway or eat by myself in the workplace cafeteria. These feelings of shame may only stop when we finally "grow up," change perspective, and see how unnecessarily paralyzing such emotions can be. These unchecked feelings would easily have kept me in a cubicle surrounded with other colleagues, just like they painfully kept me in a wrong crowd in middle school.

When I play softball, I see now how my ambivert personality reveals itself. Interestingly, having this knowledge allows me to appreciate these moments more. I watch the players, notice the commonalities and differences. I feel the pull of the extroverts standing outside the dugout and the pull of the more introverts sitting on the bench, content in their space, and I tend to sit and stand in between, sometimes going to talk outside but content in my own space or getting into more in-depth discussions.

It helps to better understand my own psychological makeup to not get pulled by its shadow side, to feel better, contribute more and with a smile. Often it's more an inner smile than outer. It's a subtle shift to become aware of this.

I watch the feeling of needing to mingle, the pressure of the social drinks after the game to "fit in." I now see it and don't get pulled by it so much, don't allow the guilt, shame, humiliation, unease, the wanting-to-be-liked to settle in. I see my frustrations, my curses, and move on. Yes, shake stuff off and move on, notice the passing summer clouds or the geese heading to the lake. In my "optimal performance flow state," I surprise the team with an unexpected catch in the deep grassy outfield.

In these moments, I experience life fully.

Like team sports, a typical workplace includes the metaphorical beer and talk. The talk is literally the talk, gossip, and ramblings, but also the deafening "cry" of the cubicle walls and the deadening environment killing creativity or flow/performance. Awareness and peace are often lost in the office hustle and bustle. The beer can be the chocolate, candy machines, coffee, whatever. The office place often has too many unproductive energy drainers. On the human side, several past colleagues always seemed to be disengaged from their work (which according to Gallup, represents over 70 percent of people) and would use me and other people to vent or mingle incessantly, while not respecting my need for focused time. I don't blame them; I probably would do the same if I were equally disengaged. The non-human aspect included the high-distraction open-concept cubicle mazes and the policies that did not allow for the scientifically proven 90-minute work cycle[18] and appropriate rests. Working from home gives the full right for creativity to flow marvellously. Working from home is being yourself in a loud manner.

Logistically, I've had appropriate support from my supervisor and virtual colleagues, with the mutual benefit of connecting through Microsoft Teams, Skype, and regular team calls to check in. I also found that tele-workers will connect amongst themselves more often, as they understand each other's specific opportunities and challenges and can offer better support. Supervisors can help by coordinating check-in calls and connecting the teleworking community.

Do you like to spend time on your own? This is probably the most important question. Are you content on your own, can you self-regulate, find peace, and re-alize the battle is about your perceptions and thoughts? Knowing this frees us from the egoic shackles that seem to always find their way in our lives. You can be both social and content on your own. You can feel like you "belong" in your team or tribe and be thousands of kilometres away. I too often hear people identifying too much on a particular attribute such as "being a very social person" and not leaving space to explore other aspects because they appear to be in conflict.

I notice how happy I am alone, where I can bask in deep gratefulness and happiness. I may enjoy other people's company, like at a campsite with old friends, and I can be at least as content when I do errands alone for two hours. It's like taking a deep breath. This same contentment can be found when I work from home, and it is always available.

I like to work on my own, and do not feel the need to connect to colleagues unless the work demands it. I prefer to work on my craft with autonomy and without direct or constant supervision. When I do have a conversation, I can enjoy it and remain open.

Meetings that last several hours or that contain high emotions can drain me for the rest of the day, and this was much worse in an office building or boardroom where I was unable to put my phone on mute and walk around, or take a quick rest to regain my focus and equilibrium. Working from home allows me to absorb the emotionally draining events more easily and remain energetic.

I can feel awkward in meetings (even if I hide this very well), but then I find my way and remain comfortable in my occasional discomforts. I often advance a discussion by being tenacious and brave in my deeper questions and intention to help.

Discipline and self-regulation are important values in life, and are especially important when working from home. I spend much of my time organizing and planning my day using Outlook Calendar and reassessing what I should prioritize. I prepare myself well, doing lists of pros and cons, asking questions that solicit the deepest directions (values, intuition). Sometimes I'll sleep on it, analyze it, but when ready, I pull the trigger. I'm still open to hearing other perspectives, but I'm not easily swayed once I conclude a well-thought-out analysis has been reached. When a decision is made, I feel the courage, energy, power of a thousand winds and currents taking me in a certain direction. It's hard to sway this. This type of conviction and intuition has been much more prevalent since I started working from home. Why? Because it is simply my natural state when my stress levels are at their optimal.

Most of the time, I am content at home doing what I love, what I am good at, what the world is asking of me through my job and being paid well for it. I am more creative, self-motivated, and enjoy my time alone. To be able to be autonomous, it helps to not care too much about what others think.

Making the transition to working from home

There are many considerations in making the transition to working from home, including personality types, level of self-control and discipline, how much you like or love your job, support from your team, family, and friends. For example, some more extroverted types may want to start with one or two days per week, but ambiverts and introverts can usually more easily jump in 100 percent. Of course, if the job you love simply can't be done at home, then probably best to stay on that path.

Working from home gives me space and removes much of the draining energy. Even if I still need to take some difficult phone calls, I at least have some distance and I don't need to answer immediately every time, not like a jolting drop-in at my cubicle, even if well-intentioned. I am better able to schedule my meetings, so I can more effectively prioritize my precious time. Combined with disciplined breaks every 90 minutes, I end my days feeling much more productive and with energy to spare.

I find more moments of autonomy and see more beauty in the world. These moments of pure awareness are disarming, relaxing, delightful, and all encompassing. I feel like this moment is enough, and it can happen anywhere in the most mundane places. Of course, the place is no longer mundane when this happens.

Working from home is an act of resilience – a spiritual act of my own autonomy. Typical workplaces may force over-socialization, when smaller doses would be preferable.

I have been an avid runner since I was fifteen, doing three marathons as well as taking part in triathlons and being a member of my university cross-country and track team. When I run, I typically do it on my own, at my own pace, at my own time as opposed to going on organized group runs. I enjoy running with others occasionally, but it's a more powerful inner experience to run alone. By working from home, I can find the same liberating feeling and I experience the deepest and most powerful way to work and live from my perspective. By knowing my own energy or pace, I can better maintain my equilibrium when I interact with others.

Just as it is much easier to be grounded and present when in nature on a beautiful day, it is also easier for me to be more grounded and present when working where I'm at my most comfortable, and taking one task at a time with no distractions – no noise, no people talking, walking, no doors closing, nor the watchful eyes of many.

By doing more in less time, I have greater stillness for myself. It's the simple little things that add up the most. A quick check-in call with my supervisor every two weeks is often sufficient to stay connected. Even this call is scheduled, and hence easier to manage in teams where distractions are prevalent.

I love how I can just "be" at home while still producing good work. Walking in nature, wandering, playing a game (even if only a few minutes), walking barefoot on grass, connecting with my dog, doing a chore (but with presence), eating healthy food – no rush, just being. How can more of this be worse than a typical office building?

Working from home will challenge you to find your autonomy. You are less hurried to beat the clock, which allows harmonious flow to your day. You aren't watched and controlled by others. These are benefits, but they also give you a new level of freedom and may open up emotions that could be uncomfortable or distracting initially. Your emotions are your own, and you are reminded to be with them, and watch them be released from their blocked pattern. Over and over this happens as you cycle through your creative chunks of time and deep renewal in a continuing process.

It helps me to share my working-from-home experiences with others who are also doing it, kind of connecting with a virtual wolf pack. I posted a blog on my workplace's intranet about my positive teleworking experience, leading me to a community of teleworkers, all sharing our stories and best practices. I got some great tips. One friend told me that "the issue is not to find the discipline to work; it's more about finding the discipline to stop working." Taking your breaks and respecting your work hours is your responsibility and you do everyone a favour by respecting this.

Working from home is a way to see that you're okay on your own, and life is good. You can be in touch with any sadness that may arise, and you can be fine with it. You don't need to be in an office or see people often; you are all right on your own. You can still contribute and be enthused every day.

To be honest, sometimes I do feel fear, or sadness, like the cry of all the people I'm not seeing in the day, a life experience I may be missing out on, as well as from being too alone. When this comes, I simply observe it and quickly realize that the here and now is enough, without all the office experience. I am enough and this is enough. Life doesn't lack anything. It takes bravery to face our fears and test the assumption that we need to see people in our workplaces on a daily basis. I find peace in the fact that life is always good, whether I fulfill my deep natural desire to connect with other humans or whether I am alone.

Office socializing can be overrated. Don't trap yourself in over-prioritizing too much social superficiality. Paradoxically, you bring more presence in your social interactions when you have more space in between, filling your soul fully and then giving the overflow to your family or other heart-filled social outings. Working from home brings a better balance of alone and social time. Alone time in a cubicle is not the same as alone at home.

This is one of the most important parts for me – my own ability to face the inevitable feeling and fear of being alone. But as mentioned, I notice the feeling, become aware of this feeling/emotion/sensation. In that moment, I am immediately able to appreciate and be grateful for all that is around me, including family, my beautiful home, being of use, and the fact that I'm wearing the clothes I want, listening to my tunes, drinking my favourite beverage, and starting the day on the right (bare) foot.

It's a different kind of social life. Old friends may make some space for new ones. You may have been asked to hold on or attach to people, things, and identities ... if it isn't working so well, best to let go and let connections happen organically. Toxic people and overburdened agendas are worth saying "no" to, and stay vigilant to keep them away. Our best lives depend on it. I find I have less of a veil and I'm less interested in the dramas of life. I am also calmer during meetings and speak more often from a place of peacefulness. Even my greeting at the start of teleconference calls has a deeper voice, and that gets noticed – my whole environment and state of mind shared in the first word from my relaxed vocal cords.

When I give public presentations, I often speak from the heart and then notice my ego trying to catch up, my psyche waking me in the middle of the night to make me feel that I shamefully "ruined it." I think the best I can offer is to look deeper and see the truth and not let these feelings lead my life. When I expose my heart, I usually don't remember all I said and never really know what I'm going to say, which seems to make the dialogues more honest and closer to the truth. At night, psyche/ego catches up to the adventurous, creative energy shining through me, bound to tear down some of our structure and norms.

During an alma mater speech I gave to first-year law school students (a school I had attended decades earlier), I spoke about my truth and path, mentioned living in the present as most important, finding work that you love, spending no more than 5 to 10 percent of your time worrying about the future, that jobs that don't yet exist are ahead, and to say yes more often at the beginning of a career. My speech was closer to dissolving the idea of a "perfect career" than solidifying it, and I sensed that my words were disrupting the trend and bringing some discomfort in a room of very career-oriented people.

For example, I mentioned the importance of considering the salary with the actual hours worked (hours divided by the salary for the true hourly pay rate), which was a clash with 60-80 hours per week lawyers sitting on the panel. Since my time in law school, I've realized that there is only now, that it's okay to create more space in my life and be open to the next opportunity not yet planned. It's okay "to change my mind," to explore, to enjoy. My passion came through. I was bold in my statements, and since my feeble psyche/ego once again felt vulnerable and exposed, I know I was probably on the right path.

It's time that more of us wake up to this modern opportunity. Large organizations are slowly going there, but with pockets of major resistance. Most employees work required hours in front of screens and rarely need face-to-face time or direct daily public interactions.

Working from home can look like wanting to be too comfortable and hiding in routine and isolation. In my experience, working from home can feel less comfortable in various psychological ways, but it's discomfort that awareness nullifies quickly. I can better handle the positive stress of meeting a reasonable deadline.

My job sometimes requires me to have conversations on complex matters with high stakes, and so it is normal to have moments of uneasiness, but I usually realize this quickly and don't project it on others (i.e., I don't constantly look to be reassured and sympathized with). I notice how I don't have the same awareness and emotional control if I'm not resting properly, like when travelling or spending several days with people with no alone time. These are the times I may start to complain and make more mistakes. When at home, I can take a deep breath whenever I need to, and focus on the tasks in my meticulously organized calendar. It is good to uplift and support each other, but ego-repairing is a fool's game, and it's best to let the ego energy dissipate or obliterate.

Which is easier done in your own working from home space.

If you don't need to be "managed," working from home is like being an entrepreneur, a sole proprietor doing your own business or following your own muse without needing to report to someone. Working from home is paradise for the driven. (See Douglas Brackmann's book *Driven*.) It's focused meaningful work with minimal residue. I'm able to renew and am less weary at end of the day (our bodies' energy cycles must be respected – we are not robots). When channelling my intensity and drive into my purpose, I'm able to self-regulate to continue the creativity and flow. I find my own optimum way to work.

There's much to be said about doing work that is meaningful. Such work can be real joy. A major cleanse.

A place we love to be. Job security helps, of course, and the fact that I maintain adequate or high performance. As grateful as I am, there are always frustrations here and there. Most work has its less enjoyable moments and I can accept that.

Of course, no job is without its mundane tasks, but when working from home these tasks feel much less burdensome and annoying. For disciplined weightlifters, when lifting heavy for one or two reps, some experts say it is best to take three or four minutes of rest doing "nothing" – which does not look "productive" to the outsider. In the office, employees are expected to "lift weights" in between the big tasks, making the power lifts much less effective. At the end of an office building day, feelings of grogginess remain. Working from home, my mind is more likely to be rested and clear, ready to be more present and less filled with the past weight of the day. I recover much better. When I am better balanced, I can much more easily get good sleep as opposed to watching just a few more minutes of some Netflix show (which turns into hours).

Working from home has the potential to open up your creative flow. For any professional, this is an important aspect to develop. From solving complex problems all the way to writing emails, doing apparently "mundane" tasks involves creativity, and all are improved with a creative mindset. This energy creates a positive, energized, relaxed atmosphere at work and at home.

Balancing working from home, FOMO, and other psychological influences

I notice I sometimes feel unhappy when I think of others who make more money than I do, or who have more experiences. I have a very strong drive for the same and they are reminders that I'm not there yet, not enough. I occasionally feel a sort of envy, light anger, grief for a loss in social connections and annoyed by current finances, always wanting more. I have a strong FOMO syndrome, Fear Of Missing Out.

These feelings of not being enough are completely cancelled when the light of awareness and acceptance shines through. My psychological "never good enough" or "never-ending improvement" is seen for how it robs the *now* for a psychological future. It always wants more, like an athlete who finished second in the Olympics. It's the same drive that makes me work from home, do intense jobs, and perform well (at least compared to many). The drive needs to be kept in check to not let it completely take hold of my awareness.

I have chosen my grind: the challenges, problems, and resistances. I could get paid more in other jobs, but that doesn't matter. I am not in it for "looks" or for what others think.

I embrace my nature, my intensity, and my seeming perfectionism. I currently work as a public servant, impartially advancing federal impact assessments for major resource projects. My drive can be blindingly intense – it had me naively saying that career is more important than family in a law school interview for a highly sought position. The drive to be a lawyer, to make lots of money, to be happy, to find bliss through doing, and to have success at doing and receiving but still striving for more, makes my spiritual and poetic awareness that much more potent. I'm particularly interested in teaching that cuts directly through my constant "searching," even without knowing I was searching.

When I am able to channel my drive toward meaningful work that makes lives better, I feel "well-used" and able to maintain perspectives on all the values I see as important. In a typical workplace, I was often seen as "very serious" because I would limit my social mingling to maintain a laser-like focus at my computer. Working from home helps me channel my drive and focus into my work, while not being distracted or needing to explain or change my more productive work method for other colleagues. I see this similar drive in people diagnosed with attention deficit or hyperactivity disorder.

Working from home may serve these people very well.[19]

I'll be honest: I have no idea where it will take me. Enormous extra space can manifest in ways we could never know – the soul relishes the ride and the process of building more presence.

One of the challenges is that I may negatively affect others in my family. For example, my wife now rarely has the house to herself to unwind, although this is easily offset by the fact that she mostly works outside of our home and she likes the fact that I'm able to do more cleaning, cooking, and being around for the kids. Although I have gained access to many more jobs by being able to telework, I may also lose on several other positions because of perceptions or actual practical reasons of not being in an office. I find the best way to challenge these perceptions is by giving all the reasons why teleworking works for me – I'm living proof that it does work. I'm fortunate to have a workplace that encourages a community of teleworkers to discuss best practices and support each other with regular calls. One high-performing colleague once said she found her best ideas and inspiration while she baked.

By running my own race, finding my own path, and staying grounded, I have been finding work that is more aligned with me. Since working from home, I have been offered better work and promotions and, as mentioned, have the energy to explore a muse or two, such as writing this book.

I may never return to an office-building type workplace. Awareness, peace, and stillness subtly follow me now, and although I am never-endingly improving and there is always more to do, I'm at peace with what I do in that moment. I now see how the maze-like cubicle environment, and those reduced human interactions, would slowly build a heavy heart, a heavy "being" with it. Today, embracing this heart and noticing stillness makes it all worth it.

Working from home is an alignment of my inner energy and outer play in life. It's noticing birdsong while running in nature on my lunch break. It's noticing my wife's angelic presence, the cute freckles on my middle daughter's face when she asks for something, or seeing the underlying peace behind my oldest's fiery desires and lioness energy. It's seeing my youngest daughter's sunny ways as she jumps from one thing to another. It's reflecting in what to do next or accessing intuition from my quiet place, to serve all.

Working from home is a pioneering stance, a perfect example of my inner creative drive, with artwork at the highest point in my office and lots of plants, rocks, grounding objects, and reminders of the infinite. I feel the dynamic tension between living the stillness and following worldly pursuits.

Working from home requires discipline and discipline equals freedom. Waking early while everyone else sleeps helps me start the day right. But like writing a book, I need the rigour/discipline to beat the clock and smell the flowers, to find my inner and outer smile before facing the day. As I wake early, I elevate my life by doing the activities (such as exercise, meditation, and learning) that nourish me and keep me energized during the day.

Indigenous Values, Well-being, and the Medicine Wheel

*Man did not weave the web of life, he is merely a strand in it.
Whatever he does to the web, he does to himself.*

– *Chief Seattle*

From 2007 until the time of writing this book, my primary work objective has been to ensure the Canadian federal government meets its constitutional obligations to consult various Indigenous Nations in Canada on proposed major resource projects. In my work with Indigenous communities, it can sometimes feel like a wild adventure, a dazzling dance between "other cultures" and Indigenous melodies, two different melodies coming together but respecting their own values like contrapuntal music. It's a dance that stays open, that does not know its next step with certainty but enjoys the ride while it lasts. To do my job well, it is important to build and maintain relationships and I like to describe it as two Nations coming together to make one beautiful polyphonic melody.

In my years of working as a public servant in the area of Indigenous consultations, I've noticed many underlying interests that rarely come to the surface, but affect what we do. If every human could come closer to a place of truth, we would probably come closer to a more heart-centred, lighter, and grounded approach. Most times, we dance at the surface of fleeting waves, rarely touching on deep-rooted matters. As meaningful as the dance may appear on the surface, it still doesn't address major, fundamental beliefs or mind and identity structures that keep egos thriving and add to the veil that blocks true connections, connections which lie closer to our source of being.

Where many would run as fast as they could in another direction, some thrive in the ambiguous. I enjoy untangling webs, intricate mazes of overlapping land claims, various electronic databases, complex project details to give listening a chance, to allow gatherings of people to listen to other gatherings. Over the years, I've been blessed to hear stories from elders that may not fit in any rigid agenda or directly relate to a specific project we are assessing, but there are elements of these stories that convey important knowledge, such as values and ways of living. The message can be communicated through words, emotions, and sometimes taste and smell like smudging (the burning of sage, sweet grass, and cedar) or traditional foods. A big part of what I do is capture this knowledge and wisdom as best I can and find the means to incorporate it in tangible ways to make better decisions.

Storytelling is extremely important in Indigenous communities, and I now have my own stories to tell from home, which rests in *Sikniktuk*, Mi'gma'gi traditional territory. *M'sit Negomag* means "all my relations" in the language spoken on this part of Turtle Island (North America) from the People of the Dawn who were living close to these lands, working in their sacred homes for more than ten thousand years.

Working from home increases and deepens *M'sit Negomag*. I am friendlier to Mother Earth, much closer to nature and natural rhythms, have more energy to choose deeper conversations and friends, and have more time to see my kids play. I have more time to watch the sun, sense the trees, and hear the birds' melodies. In fact, I have many better things in life, including better food, things the Mi'kmaq and their ancestors enjoyed and continue to enjoy after having endured so much strife from the highly unbalanced ways of European colonial newcomers.

Don't you feel so very pointless, in the feelings of the rain, and the violence of the sun. I must confess that I feel graciously bigger than the rain, and hotter than the sun.

– Ed Kowalczyk, Live (the band)

Indigenous teachings show us the importance of caring for our planet and incorporating the medicine wheel in the areas of mind, heart, body, and soul. In my work with Indigenous communities, the circle, which applies to the inner and outer life in all our relations, comes up often. Many medicine wheels have four directions and the colours white, black, red, and yellow. There are several variations of the medicine wheel and I am using the version that I have seen most often and that was explained to me by a well-respected Mi'kmaw leader.

The medicine wheel is a visual way of incorporating Indigenous knowledge into our daily lives. The wheel, colours, and teachings are found in many Indigenous communities – on buildings' signs, healing centres, artwork, and formal communications. In my experience, working from home has significantly elevated all four of these medicine wheel directions.

Working from home helps bring the balance that the medicine wheel represents. Projects can succeed or fail, processes can take time, and contracts may or may not be made. We are all human beings on this spinning Earth, forgetting often to connect to the now, the truth. Start with this. For me, rebalancing the wheel meant leaving the concrete, the cubicle lines, the mind constructs, and returning to myself, staying home, and being my best self in the world. Let's find a balanced environment to produce balanced works and creations.

Indigenous communities bring ways of being that appear ancient to the modern Western time-bound mind. It is always now and the teachings are perennial. That is one of the reasons that meetings will begin with a smudging ceremony. Music can also help bring deeper emotions to the surface, those emotions that "positive thinking" suppresses and tries to suffocate, only to have it become stuck energy that unbalances the wheel. Best to let it play through the system, be patient, and enjoy life.

There is a major wave of mental health sessions and guidance, which often show ways to cope and give a more positive feel to being in an office. These sessions are certainly beneficial, but they can sometimes feel like placing "pearls on a pig" as they rarely reach the deeper roots of the problem. For some people, working in the office building itself can be a cause for mental strife, but the sessions only touch on "coping" with the possibly toxic environment as opposed to finding a better alternative such as working from home or finding work that you love. If you already live in presence, you may live like meditation is your whole life, not just sitting on a cushion. It may happen during pockets of awareness during the day, usually when you're relatively alone and in ordinary or natural surroundings. Mental health is only one aspect of health, and one that has many dimensions, as the medicine wheel demonstrates.

Attempts are often made to release the pressures of the office building workplace energy imbalances, but they come short of sufficiently filling the spiritual, emotional, physical, and mental dimensions. My energy is not wasted in traffic, or wearing a social mask. There are few distractions and mechanical noises, and I'm no longer in an uninspiring human-made environment. I remember how removing my office clothes at the end of the day felt like removing a weight, like shedding a bunch of negative energy. I remember doing this as soon as I returned from the office – it was a great relief.

At home, I don't accumulate this "wheel warping" cortisol and bad stress/anxiety. I am paid well and spend less on car repairs, gas, clothing, and food. It's better for the planet and my personal well-being.

Since working from home, my spiritual, emotional, mental, and physical dimensions are much better balanced. Although I am focusing on four major dimensions, there are several sub-dimensions, including financial health, social health, adventure health, and impact health. I have much more peace, even amidst challenges, as well as fewer and less potent human emotional outbreaks (including my own). With fewer distractions, my mind is sharper. Meaningful work, music, or silence fuels my heart and soul. Finding a better balance does not always mean more comfort. When sharing with heart, truth, and soul, my voice sometimes shakes a bit and can feel like a vulnerable pioneer. It often feels destabilizing to leave the comfort of staying silent or staying in conformity of what's known or clinging to past mental and physical structures.

Most Western societies and office environments focus almost exclusively on the mental (head) and physical (body) aspects of the circle, and neglect the other parts of the medicine wheel. The medicine wheel reminds us to consider the spiritual (soul) and emotional (heart) aspects so we can better appreciate all of life.

I had the honour of experiencing an inspiring talk from a respected Mi'kmaw elder, Albert Marshall, who explained the importance of "two-eyed seeing" (*Etuaptmumk*), which is "learning to see from one eye with the strengths of Indigenous knowledges and ways of knowing, and from the other eye with the strengths of Western knowledges and ways of knowing ... and learning to use both these eyes together, for the benefit of all."[20]

Interestingly, the 24 values described in the first section of this book weave evenly in the four directions. I crafted a large version of this circle and placed it on my kitchen wall. Every day it reminds me and my wife to live these 24 values, to lead by example, thus teaching these values to our young daughters.

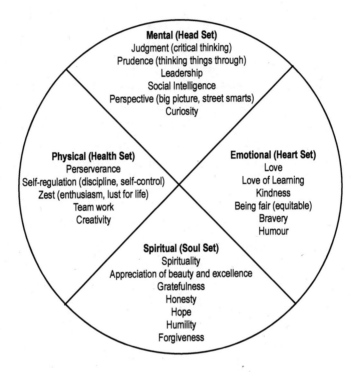

Figure 1
Weaving of Indigenous Teachings and Worldview Values

Heart Set:
The Emotional Dimension of Life

To handle yourself, use your head; to handle others, use your heart.

– Eleanor Roosevelt

The spiritual and emotional dimensions are too often forgotten or suppressed in the traditional workplace. Successful work requires building successful relationships, and that requires both the spiritual and emotional dimensions. The emotional dimension is Heart. Heart is Love. Heart is listening, feelings, connecting. The spiritual dimension is truth, the most basic truth that is seen through the eyes of awareness, not only through thoughts and past experience. When interacting with people, a response that has truth and heart is better than protecting egos or overpromising.

It helps to ask myself questions that bring more heart, truth, and presence. For example, questions like "What am I?" as opposed to "Who am I?" stir a certain contemplation, even if there is no definitive answer. I also like the questions Is this true? and What else could this mean? These deeper and impartial questions are what drive us, like a curious scientist, to see the bigger picture and perform better while maintaining our own authenticity. The questions are not meant to be answered with the mind only, but to make us live and become the answers.

Working from home allows you to metabolize your feelings, and allows them to pass more freely. You will notice emotions more in your quiet space. You will feel more spiritually and emotionally connected in all aspects of your life. Even if you feel less valued for your work – you may even be paid less – your wheel may still be better balanced. By working from home, you are also much more gentle on your physical environment – smaller carbon footprint, less air pollution – leaving you more serene, knowing you are doing your part.

I appreciate and love others in person in my daily dealings outside my work hours, and I sometimes linger a bit longer here and there, like at my kids' daycare, at the local market, or in a conversation with my family without feeling so rushed. Working from home keeps me even more grounded. I notice I don't get so pulled by everything ... and when I get caught in a web, it doesn't last so long. When "expectations" are not being met, and the emotions rise and cloud the moment, I sometimes act on the emotions and not the deeper reality beyond the emotions. The expectations are the expectations – no need to internalize them.

Below are examples of waves of thoughts, feelings, and emotions that come from time to time. Variations of these "suffering thoughts" often have their beginnings at a young age, so working from home does not necessarily create them, but can intensify them. At the same time, working from home can help you notice these "waves" more often as you sit in your own still space:

✓ Feelings of heaviness, loneliness, and a fear of missing out;

✓ Feeling of no clear distinction between work and personal life, not able to fully concentrate or rejuvenate;

✓ Feeling stalled in your career progression;

✓ Feeling you've given up on much of the world, lost your drive, are losing your social abilities and communication skills;

✓ Feeling that you will regress to a much less competent person/worker, both socially and professionally;

✓ Feeling much more vulnerable: can be more easily laid off, cut off, forgotten, or that your colleagues won't take you as seriously;

✓ Feeling that you need to hide your situation, you're too much of an outlier.

As heavy as the end of an emotional and busy day can feel, including loss of sleep and ruminating about what to do about something and all the blocked energies that come with it, when the morning comes, all can be let go at once. When I lay my head on the pillow, placing one hand on my heart, one hand on my lower abdomen, I can observe thoughts subsiding, my breathing and body energy letting go of all, allowing all to be as it is.

Here are just a few examples of things that I have accepted and forgiven myself for since I began working from home, which I think is essential to have a better emotional equilibrium:

✓ Feeling weirded out, broken, fearful, hesitant, scared, protective, controlling, isolated in a world of only abundance and beauty;

✓ For being human, for feelings of separation and suffering when it's only a psychological construct and fleeting;

✓ For missing that 20 minutes of playtime with a daughter, because of another digital distraction;

✓ For shame of anything, part of being human;

✓ For regret in posting or saying things "without thinking it through";

✓ For being conflicted;

✓ For analyzing more than needed, to a point of heart suffocation.

Emotional advantages of working from home:

✓ Can laugh or be inspired by your favourite YouTube videos on your break;

✓ Stress levels are at optimum for creative passions and performance;

✓ There's less time-guilt, attire-guilt, social-mask-guilt, shallowness-guilt, and more love and truth even if just by yourself;

✓ Can enjoy your home where you spend much of your money (mortgage or rent);

✓ Can select friends and lunch events that bring the most joy and happiness;

✓ Can let feelings settle, not smother them amongst the busy cubicle environment;

✓ There's no need for small talk, just the grand ordinary and dazzling silence (or music);

✓ Can play more, devote more time to your craft/ muse;

✓ Can spend more time with your calming pet;

✓ Overall, it's far better for the family emotional equilibrium.

The Heart Set direction has endless feelings and emotions that are often fleeting. When kept in awareness and balanced with the other directions, I find that the heart is naturally filled with a universal love and kindness, and occasionally full-out joy and enthusiasm.

Soul Set:
The Wheel's Spiritual Direction

Learn more, know less.

— *Neil Strauss*

The spiritual and soul dimension continues to be a dazzling mystery to me, and in my view is best understood by pointers, questions, and direct experience. Although there is no rigid definition, spiritual teachers often use questions like "Who am I?" and "Can I notice my breathing, inner energy, any emotions, thoughts, or any identity attached?"

For the spiritual dimension, working from home allows more awareness (or enlightenment), more time alone relishing the beauty around you, more time to just breathe. You can listen to music, be inspired by culture and the environment. You can bring a calmer voice to the workplace and society when you are working in a place closer to your authentic self.

Having awareness and enlightenment makes me more and more open, often without realizing it. It's not that I necessarily have an agenda about changing my environment or people; it's more about a deep acceptance of all, and the sail adjusts on its own to catch the full wind, and the rudder corrections are much more obvious. Interactions are very different, and I am okay with silence. I notice people who are at peace, comfortable in their own skin.

I am grateful for being alive, am conscious of my breathing. I'm even more grateful to be in awareness of it. Being in awareness automatically contains gratefulness. Being grateful requires a subtle act, a shift. This shift is a portal to awareness.

Spirituality comes naturally when I journal, especially after the thoughts are written down and stop bouncing in the psyche. Awareness shines like sunrays through clouds, even though it is always present. At home, calm, uninterrupted, I receive information at work and respond with less knee-jerk reactivity and more from my own creative force found in those quiet gaps. I'm also able to re-energize and renew by taking a break on my own time, a stroll in my home or outside to ponder the blue sky, trees, and warm air, to lay on a hammock or sit on a comfortable chair and allow it all to be as it is before stepping back into the dazzling fray of the next task on the calendar.

Awareness comes first.

In 2008, with no great fanfare, I had an awakening, and it was probably the most significant shift in my life. Once it's happened, it permeates all life at all times, and you can't go back. The ego has been managing this shift the best it can, although it doesn't have a hold like it used to. Working from home is just an experience to have, a certain path amongst many temporary and impermanent paths we choose. It's the same awareness when feeling overwhelmed in traffic or in office space when being denied promotion. Awareness is what we are. With no attached identity, it's easier to be flexible and resilient no matter the circumstances.

I try to be easy on myself. The valley of the shadow of death may or may not visit, but I am here, present, ready to experience it. How often do I notice my thoughts and emotions tormenting inside? I sometimes revert to thinking and emoting an entity, a constructed entity we may call an illusionary self. This self almost always needs "friction" to define itself better, or be seen and felt. There's no need. The greater friction of life can be felt and experienced without the added burden of a constructed self. Being in awareness and presence you see and feel life more viscerally, with less unnecessary frictions of a self trying to survive. The presence lets go of much more and any reaction or doing is done in presence, which is then not attached to as much.

The sadness or maybe loneliness I sometimes feel is one such friction that often dissolves immediately once observed. Other popular gremlins include wanting more money, more stuff, or a certain experience. My mind can always imagine having something it doesn't have, and having the associated feelings of longing, anger, jealousy, envy, and inadequacy. It's always a lesson in acceptance, all of life. Acceptance immediately dissolves the constant feeling of not having enough, not being enough, and deep unsatisfactoriness.

There still is suffering when working from home, but the suffering is worth the benefit of my own autonomy. Working from home will not likely help my ego-driven identity, but it is more likely to dissolve it if I can maintain perspective and see the bigger picture. You come closer to silence, stillness, awareness, and peace.

You don't need to choose more suffering, stuff, and titles. Now if you want this, go ahead! But I'm not the first to advise that more money, faster cars, and a bigger home will not fill the void, because this egoic void is never satisfied.

The price of working from home may mean letting go of the typical worldly success that society sells. By letting go, I am much more likely to do what feels better, to create something that resonates with me, and not stress so much about things that will not matter on my deathbed. With this "letting go" attitude, I'm paradoxically more likely to have more happiness, success, and money flowing for better life experiences.

While grinding through, I find autonomy. When things crumble earlier than predicted, the underlying life shows itself. Riding the waves of success and lists of things to do, we often forget the hidden ocean that is always present, the dazzling darkness of nothingness and everythingness (pure potentiality). We catch glimpses of awareness, if lucky enough to have realized them, like lightning flashing in the dark. We can use these flashes to see, however briefly, and they are marvellous. The flashes may increase, or not, but we can be content with both dark and light and appreciate the contrast of what we can see with our magnificent, but limited senses.

Perhaps there are many other unseen dimensions, and we are in this playground, one ground at a time, until we return to another ground. You can't truly live the play of life if you don't sometimes put in the effort to climb the slide's stairs, or push yourself to swing, and it all has its time until it may feel best to leave. Then you're content to return to the walk back, and content with whatever pops up in the now.

Ways to access the Spiritual Direction while working from home:

- Embrace silence;
- Listen to birds, watch the clouds, the horizon;
- Step outside, ground yourself, and fill your soul in one deep breath;
- Smile internally (for your true self, and not only for others);
- Take back your life – you chose your work, it doesn't rule you;
- Hide the clock;
- Have longer breaks; have flexible, adaptable days;
- Play games with your kids before work, during breaks;
- Watch your kids wake from their sleep;
- In phone conversations, listen without always thinking of your next answer;
- Revel in your music, your food, your warm tea;
- Have a short nap on break, or meditate;
- Be content with simplicity, be content with "less."

A healthy Soul Set is easy to accomplish, yet it is often neglected. It is as simple as remembering to take deep breaths during the day and noticing the present moment. For me, taking a mid-day walk outdoors (e.g. walking in nature with my dog) refills my soul so I can be better balanced for the rest of the day.

Head Set:
The Mental Direction

Happiness does not bring gratefulness. Gratefulness brings happiness.

> *– David Steindl-Rast, Benedictine monk*

Of all the four directions, the Head Set is probably the one we can most readily associate with our working lives. The Head Set is also where there appears to be most potential drawbacks[21] such as increased isolation and a potentially unhealthy blend of work and personal life. However, with a good set of ground rules and discipline, the advantages can often far outweigh the drawbacks, such as an increased sense of control, flexibility, escaping the office's social dynamics, and spending more uninterrupted time focused on your craft.

According to the Canadian Mental Health Association, "Mental illness indirectly affects all Canadians at some time through a family member, friend or colleague" and "In any given year, 1 in 5 people in Canada will personally experience a mental health problem or illness."[22]

Mental health is one of the most significant concerns I hear about regarding working from home, where there is less social interaction and support from colleagues. The Government of Canada defines mental illness as "the reduced ability for a person to function effectively over a prolonged period of time because of:

- significant levels of distress
- changes in thinking, mood or behaviour
- feelings of isolation, loneliness and sadness
- the feeling of being disconnected from people and activities"[23]

In conversations I've had with other teleworkers, social isolation is mentioned as the most significant drawback. This is often indicated in studies as well. In a typical office, the social aspect is automatically structured into the workday. However, this potential drawback can be countered by scheduling your own preferred quality social time, such as:

✓ Spend more time with the people you love at home;

✓ Make an effort to connect online (ideally video, such as Skype, Zoom, or Microsoft Teams) with colleagues and other work-related people;

✓ Participate in work activities that bring you out of the house;

✓ Spend some days at the office building workplace (e.g. every Friday);

✓ Book a weekly lunchtime walk or coffee with a good friend;

✓ Make an extra effort to show up and participate in your family's social activities;

✓ Join a gathering of your interest, such as a cooking class, a sports team, or civic engagement.

For some, these activities may not sufficiently replace the often high amount of in-person social activities in an office building. However, for many, the right amount of quality social activity will be more fulfilling than higher amounts but lower-quality social encounters. The amount of social activity you may feel you need to schedule varies depending on your own psychological makeup and perceived needs. For me, a good face-to-face conversation with a friend is worth days of more superficial trivialities in the workplace kitchenette.

I believe working from home can improve mental health, unless you are already affected by a mental health challenge, in which case a qualified professional may understandably recommend more social interaction, including a typical office building environment. Mental health issues may also develop over time regardless of the place we work, and I think this is always something to be aware of and to seek help from a medical professional when needed.

Mental health is a complicated subject that varies significantly for each person. I am immensely grateful to have a close partner (wife) and family who support me immensely, and I suspect that maintaining close relationships may be a key factor for most people's success for a long-term working-from-home experience.

For the mental quadrant, by working from home my mind has become more clear, focused, and relaxed. I am able to find the zone (or flow) more often in the day with less distraction. I am better and more frequently able to notice my endless mental noise or any emotional turmoil in my serene work space. Feelings like isolation, loneliness, sadness, or feeling disconnected from people and activities will often loosen or disappear just by noticing.

Human interaction and conversation are exquisite experiences, but are thwarted by us wanting to be heard before listening to others and ourselves. The environment and state of mind matter, the fertile ground for good conversations. A phone conversation done from your home brings great discussion with no constraints, lots of smiles/laughs and connection, and no guilty feelings that your voice will disrupt other people's workspaces (I tend to talk and laugh loudly).

I often hear others say they need to work a few days at home to get away from distractions and finish some big piece of work. Their workplaces have their own pull in a whirlwind of disruptions that are much more difficult to control than at home. It's human nature to avoid the difficult tasks, those that require our full attention, because it can be highly taxing on our system. Every other diversion is an easy way out for the more difficult tasks, and other people are one of the greatest pulls of distraction. Working only a few days as opposed to 100 percent from home may not sufficiently remove the gravitational pull of distractions and guilt to have the full benefits. It is also highly inconvenient, time-consuming, and draining if you need to carry all your stuff from one place to the other, and easy to forget items, especially at the end of a busy and exhausting day.

* * *

Working from home is a re-grounding. However, weekends and vacations are also important for renewals in other ways, such as renewal of the heart and soul with less mind. This is especially true if these times are filled with activities that fill you with good energy (contentment, joy, rest) as opposed to more burdensome tasks that drain you too much.

Mental advantages of working from home:

✓ Able to take on lots of work more effectively and efficiently and with mind-energy to spare at the end of the day;

✓ Can use your days fully, less wasted time;

✓ Can escape the office's social dynamics, such as distractions of unnecessary meetings, social gatherings, or unscheduled chats at the water cooler;[24]

✓ Creates distance from more difficult or toxic personalities, making it easier to objectively complete the required tasks;

✓ Much less distracted by other people's agendas or activities in a typical cubicle environment, giving free rein to love and truth in the vast psyche, your inner self;

✓ Better concentration, even if others are in the home (e.g. cleaning services, pets);

✓ Fewer decisions to make, which increases capacity to make better decisions;

✓ Less stress and more exercise, allowing greater production of high-performance natural chemicals such as dopamine and less of the stifling cortisol.

The silence I cherish once the world leaves to their workplaces or schools is like a reset, a return to source – my whole body shivers and hums at this silent celebration. It is a powerful reminder that I try to remember daily. I have my thoughts, to-do lists, electronic calendar, emails, and documents to process much of my day, but I try to remember to return to source at 90-minute intervals, giving me the renewal needed to tackle the next block of time. In the end, it's remembering to remember that life is good and that you are much more than your unpredictable thoughts and emotions.

Health Set:
The Physical Direction

The only way to deal with an unfree world is to become so absolutely free that your very existence is an act of rebellion.
— *Albert Camus*

Work is an opportunity to ground ourselves in the physical human experience. Working from home gives you more control to have deep, focused work, with adequate rest and renewal, and is simply a more harmonious way to spend your limited time on our strange rock called Earth.

I worked for more than a decade in a cubicle environment, where I grew tremendously in experience and knowledge, but I was always attracted to the idea of not being bound by an office building and cubicle walls. The policies, technology, and security in my workplace have been in place since at least 2010, but teleworking remains rare, just as the electric cars and renewable energy have been slow at replacing fossil fuels. This could be the next big key to recruitment, retention, and improved work satisfaction.

One potential drawback in the physical direction is developing bad eating habits, given the easy availability of food only a few seconds away. To help manage this, I cook healthy meal batches on Sundays that last the week. *The 4-Hour Chef* by Tim Ferriss has helped me eat healthier by cooking for a "slow carb diet," eating less, and having, as mentioned, healthy, pre-made meals during work time.

Many experts recommend exercising intensely three times per week. With the extra energy and time you gain by working from home, you can go for a run or bike ride on lunch breaks without worrying about needing to immediately shower or having your bike stolen. You can do weight-bearing activities in your home office (push-ups, planks, burpees) without wasting precious lunchtime minutes commuting to a fitness club (I guess I also save on gym membership costs and needing to change clothes).

Some activities help many dimensions of health concurrently. From home, you can go for runs/walks at a more convenient time and are able to organize your whole life, including your personal matters, along with meditating, watching inspirational videos on YouTube, listening to invigorating music, or lighting cleansing incense.

The stress load is much lower with no commute in traffic, no lunch to prepare in a frenzy, no choosing specific clothes or shaving or cleaning shoes, no car not starting or snow to clear. It's just you, your warm beverage, and a music or comedy video all after calmly bringing kids to the bus stop or feeding your pet. By working from home, you'll probably live longer, be healthier, and look younger.

I highly recommend waking up early, eating well, and exercising regularly to fully benefit.

Physical advantages of working from home (from the Health Set perspective):

- No more daily traffic, and no more needing to leave before rush hour;
- Errands or appointments can be done at more convenient times when there's less traffic and less time wasted by things like taking an elevator or finding parking;
- Can take longer walks with the dog, with no social mask (dressed however you want);
- It justifies buying or renting a better home but in a more affordable area, such as the outskirts of town. You can spend more on mortgage or rent, and less on other items like transportation. A tip: Many baby boomers have homes for sale or rent. Look for a suitable office room, with a door and good lighting;
- You're always home with your family at the end of the day;
- Can do small house chores each day that can free up your weekends;
- Enjoy your own, allergen-free space, and move within it however you like.

The Practices:
How to work from home successfully – For personal success and professional success

All change is hard at first, messy in the middle and gorgeous at the end.

– Robin Sharma

Even before COVID-19, several studies indicated that more and more people were teleworking or working from home. While there are many obvious advantages, I often hear people and news articles say that working from home is a source of unhappiness and mental health issues. Yet this observation fails to ask a more important and fundamental question of whether these same people enjoy the work they do from home most of the time.

The Gallup organization finds that 70 percent of U.S. workers are not engaged at work[25] and do it almost solely for the pay. I suspect that these same people likely use workplace social interactions as a buffer to distract from their feelings or from doing the unfulfilling work, whether they realize it or not. If the work does not ignite a sense of purpose and meaning, that can be a major cause of suffering, and working from home may intensify the suffering by removing the social interactions that nourish the soul just enough to make the gruelling work bearable, kind of like group therapy.

In other words, it matters that you at least like what you do most of the time. Working from home successfully is not about escaping your work, but more about diving more deeply in your work that you already like and improving your overall health and happiness. If you try to work from home at a job that depletes you too often, you will likely still feel depleted working from home. And on top of that, you'll lose the support (or welcomed distraction) of co-workers who kept your spirits up before.

Why does working from home work for some but not others? Is it about loving your work, being more of an introvert, having strong supportive relationships at work and at home, having a suitable workplace at home? Or is it a combination of all of these? Does working from home increase your health set, head set, heart set, and soul set? I think that the more these four fundamental directions are improved by working from home, then the more your life satisfaction and happiness will improve in a sustainable manner. For some disengaged employees who may be struggling in their teleworking arrangement, a change in work may be what they need more than a return to a cubicle.

Ikigai: The formula for personal and professional success

Few people are comfortable alone.

– Douglas Brackmann, PhD

Your escalation requires your isolation.

– Robin Sharma, The 5 AM Club

How much more presence would be felt and lived if more people worked from home, bringing much more "being" to the human "doings" of the world? To figure out your right livelihood – the work in which you can feel fully free to access the Four Directions – we can turn to the Japanese concept of Ikigai.

Work – what we do for a living – brings a brilliant opportunity to love others, to listen, make new connections, and thrive. On page 90 is a diagram for Ikigai, the Japanese term for "a reason for being." Working from home can help in all four circles of the Ikigai, including helping you love where you work and what you do, bringing more balance to your Ikigai, and more delight and fullness.

Similar to the medicine wheel, the Ikigai diagram is a simple compass to help find imbalances and guide you to a better way to spend your days. For example, you probably know professionals who are good at what they do and get paid well but don't enjoy their work, have trouble finding meaning, and may feel empty. Finding a better balance would mean exploring whether the opposite circles could be incorporated to bring more balance, which could be just a few tweaks or a complete job or career change.

Work is love made visible.

– Kahlil Gibran

WHAT MAKES LIFE WORTH LIVING

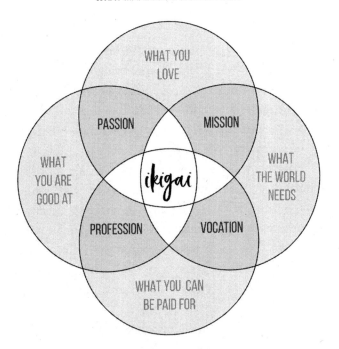

THE PROCESS OF ALLOWING
THE SELF'S POSSIBILITIES TO BLOSSOM

Figure 2 The four dimensions of Ikigai.
(Source: iStock by Getty Images)

Once our Ikigai is found, work may feel more like play. Does it matter if how we spend our days can't be easily named or placed on an organizational chart? I prefer to focus on the work and discipline and not a predetermined career path or profession. Work is an opportunity to love others. It's a way to spend our time on this glorious blue planet.

In order to work more productively, I use Outlook Calendar to organize chunks of uninterrupted time. One block of time can be more productive than a whole day dealing with the urgent but less important tasks. These chunks of time, interspersed with breaks (even if only a two-minute mindfulness walk to the bathroom), at 90-minute intervals, are exponentially more powerful and potent for getting the right things done.

* * *

In Canada, the federal government is the nation's largest employer, and usually offers security of job, pension, and benefits. I'm grateful to have been a public servant since 2004. I find most public servants are hard-working and make a genuine effort to improve people's lives. I wonder if this attitude comes in part from a higher level of job security than experienced in the private sector. If you have relatively high job security, you have fewer emotional roller coasters. This solid foundation can contribute to increased confidence, thus launching you toward greater performance.

Working from home can provide a similar foundation, regardless of your employer. It affords you the freedom to expand your job options as you're not bound by what's offered in your town or city. By enjoying your job more, you balance all wheel directions and are likely to perform better, be happier, and exude a contagious enthusiasm for your work that makes you more attractive to hiring managers. Since working from home, I've gotten more job offers and promotions than ever before. Performance is what should matter in the eyes of employers and I have demonstrated that I perform better at home.

Between 2003 and 2016, I spent most of my work days in office buildings and cubicles, and learned much about office environments. I enjoy my work – solving issues and making lives better – and I enjoy doing it from home, building my writing and creative juices every day. I resonate deeply with the values of Indigenous communities that I work with, including creativity and balance. Being closer to the ground naturally brings this.

To counter the status quo, businesses could create policies that would level the power balance by allowing employees to request working from home. This request could only be denied if there was substantial demonstration that it would not be possible in terms of performance and operational requirements. There is not much knowledge work that can't be done when you have access to a phone, the Internet, and suitable workspace. This would demonstrate the employer's support by making it easier for an employee to submit a request and at least pressure the employer to give good reasons why it would not work. There is also a need for guidance to both employers and employees to better understand what it takes to make teleworking successful and how performance will be executed and evaluated. (Since COVID-19, this guidance has increased exponentially and you can find some of it in the Recommended Resources section at the end of this book.)

I remember being intrigued by the teleworking aspect of Blueprint 2020, which was launched in 2013. A recent Beyond 2020 and public service renewal[26] framework focuses on "mindsets and behaviours" in a time that is "increasingly characterized by data, digital, new workplace designs, flatter work cultures, and multiple generations working together."[27]

By working from home, you can strategically schedule tasks and ignore office distractions so you can better prioritize your precious time.

Indigenous teachings show us the importance of caring for our planet and incorporating the medicine wheel in all we do, including our health set, head set, heart set, and soul set. Working from home can significantly elevate all four of these medicine wheel directions and I believe teleworking should be more prominently promoted for a more agile, more inclusive, and better-equipped Public Service for the next generations.

Negotiating a better life

There is no need to leave your job, and you can start with one day per week of working from home. For me, it was a complete full-time changeover while still having the option of returning to the office building. Although I felt the need to perform more to prove it worked in the early days, I have easily improved the way I work.

The Canadian federal government has a solid telework policy[28] with the following preamble:

The Treasury Board, as Employer of the Public Service, is committed to providing policies and provisions designed to help employees balance their work, personal, and family responsibilities. In keeping with our goal of being a workplace of choice, this policy will assist in meeting both business and sustainable development objectives while satisfying the growing needs of employees to improve their overall quality of life.

Changes are occurring in the Public Service workforce with a shift towards more knowledge workers, as well as changes to traditional family structures, employees' expectations of work, and the definition of career aspirations and job satisfaction.

Flexibility in the workplace to accommodate work, personal and family needs can result in benefits to organizations such as:

- *a competitive edge for attracting and retaining highly skilled individuals*
- *reduced levels of employee stress and conflict;*
- *higher levels of productivity and reduced absenteeism;*

- *higher levels of employee satisfaction and motivation;*
- *a more satisfying work environment;*
- *ability to accommodate employment related needs for employment equity designated group members.*

The impact of flexible work arrangements can also reach beyond the benefits derived by the organization and contribute to the development of a sustainable society. For example, opportunities for reducing traffic congestion and air pollution and for supporting regional economic development can be realized at the same time the employer's objectives are met.

Both managers and employees are responsible to ensure that operational needs of the organization are met and that neither productivity nor costs are negatively impacted by the application of this policy.

Teleworking agreements lay out the specific weekdays for remote work and include termination clauses which reduces the manager's risk if the employee does not perform or meet organizational requirements. In the beginning and to help with buy-in, it may be preferable to have a tryout period with weekly check-in calls to gauge whether the arrangement is working. After a few weeks, the employee and manager may already see positives outweighing any drawbacks, especially when the performance is at least as good as in the office building and that the employee is happier overall. If not, then at least you had the experience and may have learned something about yourself without needing to leave your workplace.

Energy management

As mentioned earlier, working from home helps by giving you more control of your schedule, allowing you to be dressed comfortably, ready for a walk in the sun or relaxing on a hammock during a break. I am highly organized at work, which helps keep my mind flexible and fluid enough to avoid the frazzle/draining effect. Much of my time is spent on my calendar, not my inbox (which I generally only check two or three times per day). I constantly reorganize my calendar/schedule and pick more difficult tasks in the morning, when my energy is at its best.

Energy on a Friday is often different than other workdays. Working from home helps manage this, where I can better organize lighter tasks (important, but not urgent) on a Friday, like doing data logging, phone calls, and a lunch date with a colleague.

Working from home means no strain of getting prepared in the morning, no commute, and no pretending with colleagues at work. In an office building, I am almost forced to be more social and work less. Distractions were much more difficult to ignore in the typical workplace environment. I get much more done when working from home, and feel much better about it.

Once immersed in tasks, usually using screens, does it really matter where I do it? The rest in between these intense bouts is just as important. For me, small talk or gossip in the hallways is not restful or rejuvenating. Working from home allows more of these flow moments, and to have the optimal and more tailored oscillation between performance and rest.

A Meditation on the Wider Social and Environmental Implications and Possibilities of Working From Home

Noticing the Quiet or your breath is noticing the meditation that is already happening without trying to meditate, it's a meditation in itself.

— *Adyashanti*

Live your life with a touch of rascal-ness.

— *Alan Watts*

Working from home is a strong statement to the world and to your soul that you matter, that concentration matters, that you are autonomous, comfortable in your own skin, a contributor but not an energy drainer, that you care for your health in all ways and with all your relations. Alone but not lonely, you are willing to dive deeper than social norms, into your fear, your own daily sufferings, and negative emotions. You are. You are, and that is enough. The comforts of the office may be an illusion for you; home may be where the real comfort is.

It is now undeniable that humans are harming our tiny, spectacular planet at an alarming pace. Protecting the environment should come first. Working from home often feels like a way to at least stop contributing to the demise. Freed from shackles, you may feel like you're flying, freely choosing to work for the service of others. In the history of humanity, cubicles are a very new concept, created decades before the Internet existed. Alone time is critical to your creativity, productivity, balance, and well-being. It all comes together, it's all interconnected. If you're a sensitive person, you may experience things more intensely and open offices can drive you crazy. Author Travis Bradberry indicates that in these cases, "your sensitivity to other people, loud noises, and other stimuli makes it practically impossible for you to work effectively in an open-office environment. You're better off in a cube or working from home."[29]

Sensitive people can often be compared to highly tuned antennas, essentially picking up all the energy from their environment. Working from home helps such "frequency holders" maintain a more calming and peaceful demeanour, creating from our better place to overcome all that we lose in our daily unsatisfactoriness of a thousand things – the expectations, the lust, greed, anger and fear, the pursuit of happiness, of pleasure, of thrill – all those unhealthy dopamine addictions. Just one thread of this enticing human vortex pulls you in deeper and off you go again and again. The frequency holder is able to put an end to being sucked into the vortex and instead sees the vortex and can inner-smile at it, be in awareness of it, and balance it to the point that they may feel like they're completely out of the vortex, or peacefully in the centre of it.

For all the perceived downsides and weird emotions you may initially get from working from home, even in "normal" non-pandemic times, what you gain in personal sovereignty and peace of mind may override them all. I don't need to go to an office, or a jet plane, or a car to live well, be content. I can find enthusiasm and enjoyment at home. I may find contentment and happiness more often because my frequency attracts it much more often. My inner world is in another realm, a more natural state so that I have a better relationship with the outer. Holding this natural state is much more difficult when dealing with other people or driving in city traffic. Like walking in nature or climbing mountains, working from home is an easier place to be aware. I remember the shared office toilet being my almost only place for re-grounding because it was the only door I could lock. However, the planet has infinitely better places than a smelly office bathroom to find peace.

Without the need to worry so much about someone else's flavour-of-the-day vision or mission, I look inwards. For practical purposes, it helps to have good habits and routines for physical activity, meals, chores, and work hours. Wanting more stuff may not go away, even when I already have lots of it. But it's an ever-changing thing and I find myself more focused about being grateful for what I already have. It's great when you can achieve and see what life is like and realize that suffering will continue until you STOP and smell the roses, and be content. Experiencing different settings gave me a richer contrast and I am better able to appreciate working from home.

Due to a lack of maturity in all realms of the medicine wheel, I would not have been ready for it in my first years of employment.

But without fanfare or major external changes, there was a major internal shift. I was ready when opportunity came, like a ripe fruit that is more easily detached from its branch, autonomous in its new direction even if it appears "less connected" to the inexperienced eye. What a wonderful paradox – you are more connected by appearing more disconnected, more free by not leaving home.

A "retired" person will not typically miss their office cubicle. They'll often continue working but take more breaks and do what they now love – whether getting paid for it or just as a hobby. Working from home gives you a piece of what retirement offers, more space for your creativity to flourish.

It's human tendency to want to connect, and there are different ways to do it. Workplace social is often not the kind of social that we most need. It is plagued with trivialities, superficial discussions, constant and exhausting social masks, unofficial dress codes. Your energy intermingles with other people's anxieties and unconscious energies that scream for immediate attention.

Social media and social events, if left unchecked, quickly become too much of a good thing. Again, I'm not saying "hermiting" is better, but it's best to cherish those alone moments and be comfortable in your own skin. You are enough! Of course, when feeling a bit too out of touch, it's good to connect with others and not just stay home watching screens. It's good to have other activities, or hobbies. If you don't have healthy routines, if you eat poorly or often lack sleep, working from home will feel emotionally heavier, but this would also likely be felt in any other work arrangement. And it's good to call a friend to go for a lunch walk, or call an old co-worker to chat on a Friday afternoon.

We're not alone in this working from home journey, and whether you're contemplating working from home or you've being doing it for years, you can find nuggets of knowledge and pointers in many places to craft a better life and make lives better. Living this way has its challenges, its angst and fears but journalling, sharing, and being grateful for all the advantages will help you appreciate this path much more. Living as more of an outlier, your best life, or maybe any life, usually means having all these paradoxical energies at the same time. Let's keep moving forward.

We all appreciate each other much more for being brave. It inspires us to look deeper, to not take things too seriously, and that work is an opportunity to love others and make lives better, including yours.

Keeping a journal about your working-from-home experience has many benefits, even more when having different competing emotions with less people to share them with. Let your emotions out on paper when starting the day, and you'll see them burn up in awareness.

One way to start is with a list of what you're grateful for, perhaps all the great things working from home brings.

One of my favourite teachers and authors, Adyashanti,[30] talks about the paradox of unity and spiritual autonomy. He talks of redemptive love, which we bring when we find the source in all (both the everythingness and nothingness), and at the same time our own unique point of awareness and autonomy, and how they both matter, and how we bring things closer to their natural state when we find our own ground of being.

Working from home is the perfect in-between world of doing and being. Working in an office building makes the "doing" much louder and the "being" more elusive, often killing creativity in the process. We can easily "be" when alone in a comfortable home, with control of the temperature, a comfortable chair, a sunny spot. And then, like picking up a writing pad on a Caribbean beach, you turn on your laptop, listen to elevating music, and log into the online system, drinking tea and wearing shorts. There aren't 100 decisions between you and your place of creativity/home. You remain in your optimal zone more often, and stay away from high anxiety.

M'sit Negomag, "all my relations" in the ancient words of the Mi'kmaq who journeyed and worked on the lands where I write these words. The transcendent sky I see as I write this brings me back to the original perspective, reminds me of the source that we are, of the opportunities we have, of the now we are in, of the interconnectedness of all.

There is no better time than now. Whether we feel more needs to happen or we feel something too debilitating has happened, the truth is always now, and we are blessed when we can have this realization. There is no going back. Meditation honours the now, like being in awareness of your family or friends' energies. Physical exercise honours this, bringing numerous benefits to your body. One will never find a better time to connect this inner message with other beings. Conscious living remains overly elusive for probably billions; what an opportunity to share a life-changing gift even if just in your immediate surroundings. Now is always a good time.

Potential tipping points (pandemics and other emergencies)

In early 2020, the coronavirus (COVID-19) pandemic forced millions to work from home. These types of situations make working from home more difficult, even for the more seasoned teleworkers. The exceptional times of isolation and social distancing make work very difficult for many, like when needing to care for dependants or not having the suitable work environment and tools. This type of "forced" remote work is not the ideal "test" to know if working from home is preferable, as there may be too many other stressors that blur the advantages. However, as weeks turn into months and normality and balance return, I suspect that those who find their peace and flow will often not want to return to their usual office building as quickly and should therefore seriously consider continued teleworking where possible.

The silver lining may be that a tipping point is crossed where enough people want to continue teleworking to significantly change the way we think about our work environments and reduce Green House Gas (GHG) emissions to save us from climate catastrophes. GHG reductions in China were quickly noticed by NASA satellite images within weeks of the Wuhan lockdown and reductions in fossil fuel burning. Will enough of us be able to continue working in a way to rebalance ourselves and our planet?

Conclusion

The greatest threat to our planet is the belief that someone else will save it.

– Sir Robert Swan

This book has become a passion, and I hope I can help others by sharing my experience. I am an experiment, a human guinea pig, like many others. Before COVID-19, a Buffer survey of 2,500 teleworkers[31] found that remote work is not only a trend, but here to stay with 99 percent of respondents indicating that "they would like to work remotely at least some of the time for the rest of their careers."

My own workplace, since I started, now has many more people working from home. I've also helped recruit high-performing and happy teleworkers. According to the 2017 State of Telecommuting in the U.S. Employee Workforce Report and a survey by Global Workplace Analytics and FlexJobs[32], telecommuting (those non-self-employed people who principally work from home at least half-time) grew 91 percent between 2005 and 2017 in the United States. That translates to

4.7 million workers, or more than 3 percent of the total U.S. workforce and an increase from 3.9 million in 2015. A TalentLMS Remote Work Survey[33] found that 85 percent of remote workers say that remote work was their decision because they wanted more flexibility, to make their own hours, and to live a carefree lifestyle, and that 88 percent would recommend a remote-work career.

When I'm on phone calls with colleagues, they often notice birds chirping in the background. I suspect several are a little envious, and I imagine another frazzled office day like those days when, instead of decompressing at home immediately after shutting off the work computer, I'd get a stress-inducing drive in traffic and then arrive home more emotionally drained. Today I find myself in a much better state of mind, body, heart, and soul to be present with my wife, who continues to work in a typical office building, usually by being the first to ask "How was your day?"

We reduce cubicles and cut the phone cords. It's one step short of a much bigger potential of making high-performing employees less distracted, more fulfilled, better performing, and economically advantageous (both to the organization and personally). In addition, there's a smaller carbon footprint when working remotely.

I found a pot of gold, but it's not just for me – it's for many knowledge workers. We have this choice thanks to the technology developed with a lot of human effort and innovation, and it's available in our rich world. Stop and embrace it! There is no certainty and even I may change directions depending on the opportunity and whether my working from home days become more about "accepting" than enjoying. However, it is much more likely that my work will continue from home, regardless of what that work or Ikigai may be, and how much Artificial Intelligence has evolved to replace most of our "work."

As I grow in my career and professional life, working from home has given me a new sense of autonomy. This has been a significant change for my outer and inner worlds. It may last for the rest of my public service career, or may not. In the meantime, I enjoy this new playground perspective immensely, and I hope a great many more people can also find this holy grail of playgrounds for their Ikigai, health set, head set, heart set, and soul set so they can enjoy an overall harmonious and better life.

Endnotes

1. *Shared Virtue: The Convergence of Valued Human Strengths Across Culture and History* by Katherine Dahlsgaard, Christopher Peterson, Martin E.P. Seligman, First Published September 1, 2005. https://ppc.sas.upenn.ed/sites/default/files/strengthsacrosshistory.pdf

2. *Find Your F*ckyeah: Stop censoring who you are and discover what you really want.* Alexis Rockley. 2019. Chronicle Prism.

3. inc.com/scott-mautz/a-2-year-stanford-study-e=shows-astonishing-productivity-boost-of-working-from-home.html

4. remote.co/10-stats-about-remote-work/

5. See Brigitte Racine's adaptation of Dr. Russell Barklay's method at: educoeur.ca/le-truc-du-mois-le-temps-desclusivite/

6. See *Emotional Intelligence 2.0* by Travis Bradberry and Jean Greaves. 2009. Talent Smart.

7. *Oxford English Dictionary* defines remote as "situated far from the main centres of population; distant." In this case, remote is meant to be a location away from a workplace where other colleagues regularly work on a daily basis.

8. See 7 Work-at-Home Ground Rules to Boost Your Productivity at: thebalancecareers.com/work-at-home-ground-rules-to-boost-your-productivity-4140219

9. According to the article "The five keys to a successful Google team," higher psychological safety "affects pretty much every important dimension we look at for employees." See: rework.withgoogle.com/blog

10. 6 Clever Ways to Take a Mid-Day Break (blog post): thebalancecareers.com/clever-ways-to-make-a-mid-day-break-4136299

11. 8 Reasons for Working at Home (blog post): thebalancecareers.com/reasons-for-working-at-home-3542568

12. As described by the Corporate Finance Institute, the term "knowledge worker" was first coined by Peter Drucker in his book *The Landmarks of Tomorrow* (1959). Drucker defined knowledge workers as high-level workers who apply theoretical and analytical knowledge, acquired through formal training, to develop products and services. He noted that knowledge workers would be the most valuable assets of a 21st-century organization because of their high level of productivity and creativity.

13. According to the Global Rich List, a $32,400 annual income will easily place American schoolteachers, registered nurses, and other modestly salaried individuals among the global 1% of earners.

14. According to the *Encyclopedia of Buddhism*, "Samsāra (Sanskrit, Pali; also sasāra) is commonly translated as 'cyclic existence,' 'cycle of existence,' etc. It can be defined as the continual repetitive cycle of birth and death that arises from ordinary beings' grasping and fixating on a self and experiences (...) Samsāra arises out of *avidya* (ignorance) and is characterized by *dukkha* (suffering, anxiety, dissatisfaction). In the Buddhist view, liberation from samsāra is possible by following the Buddhist path" (see: encyclopediaofbuddhism.org/wiki/Samsara).

15. Center for Applications of Psychological Type Research Services in 1996 sampled 914,219 people and found that 49.3 percent were extroverts and 50.7 percent were introverts.

16. *Driven: Understanding and harnessing the genetic gifts shared by entrepreneurs, Navy SEALS, pro athletes, and maybe you.* Douglas Brackmann, PhD. 2017. Lioncrest Publishing.

17. The bystander effect can be attributed to "Social psychologists Bibb Latané and John Darley who popularized the concept of the bystander effect following the infamous murder of Kitty Genovese in New York City in 1964 (...)." (psychologytoday.com/ca/basics/bystander-effect)

18. In *The Power of Full Engagement*, Tony Schwartz and Jim Loehr describe the 90 to 120 minutes ultradian rhythms as discovered, in the early 1950s, by researchers Eugene Aserinsky and Nathan Kleitman for sleep cycles, and with further research in the 1970s were demonstrated to also apply in our waking lives.

19. additudemag.com/adhd-career-why-work-from-home/

20. See Elder Albert Marshall's Guiding Principle of Two-Eyed Seeing and how it is applied at: integrativescience.ca/Principles/TwoEyedSeeing/. See video at: integrativescience.ca/Media/Video/

21. See balancecareers.com for more information on reasons to work from home and potential drawbacks.

22. cmha.ca/fast-facts-about-mental-illness

23. canada.ca/en/public-health/services/about-mental-illness.html

24. 8 Reasons for Working at Home (blog post) – thebalancecareers.com/reasons-for-working-at-home-3542568

25. news.gallup.com/poll/180404/gallup-daily-employee-engagement.aspx

26. canada.ca/en/privy-council/topics/blueprint-2020-public-service-renewal.html

27. ibid

28. tbs-sct.gc.ca/pol/doc-eng.aspx?id=12559

29. forbes.com/sites/travisbradberry/2016/08/30/9-signs-youre-a-highly-sensitive-person/#18f469e962e3

30. See Adyashanti.org or YouTube for a treasure trove of free and life-changing Adyashanti videos and books.

31. buffer.com/state-of-remote-work-2019

32. flexjobs.com/blog/post/flexjobs-gwa-report-remote-growth/

33. talentlms.com/blog/remote-work-statistics-survey/

Recommended Resources

Online tests for working from home compatibility:
https://www.talentlms.com/blog/remote-work-statistics-survey/
www.leadershipiq.com/blogs/ leadershipiq/84146945-quiz-is-your-personality-suited- to-working-remotely-or-in-the-office.

Telework and Home Office Health and Safety Guide
– Canadian Centre for Occupational Health and Safety -
https://www.ccohs.ca/products/publications/telework.html

Telework Policy for the Government of Canada -
https://www.tbs-sct.gc.ca/pol/doc-eng.aspx?id=12559

Going Remote Guide - https://busrides-trajetsenbus.ca/en/going-remote-guide/

Adyashanti. *Falling Into Grace.* 2011 (Sounds True, Inc.)

Aurelius, Marcus. *Meditations.* 2006 (Penguin Classics)

Bradberry, Travis and Jean Greaves. *Emotional Intelligence 2.0.* 2009 (TalentSmart)

Buckingham, Marcus. *Go Put Your Strengths to Work: 6 Powerful Steps to Achieve Outstanding Performance.* 2007 (Free Press)

Buckingham, Marcus. *Stand Out: The Groundbreaking New Strengths Assessment from the Leader of the Strengths Revolution.* 2011 (Thomas Nelson)

Cain, Susan. *Quiet: The power of introverts in a world that can't stop talking.* 2013 (Random House)

Dyer, Wayne. *The Power of Intention.* 2004. Hay House Inc.

Ferriss, Timothy. *The 4-Hour Chef: The Simple Path to Cooking Like a Pro, Learning Anything, and Living the Good Life.* 2012 (New Harvest)

Gibran, Kahlil. *The Prophet.* 1951 (Vintage Books, Penguin Random House LLC)

Kahneman, Daniel. *Thinking Fast and Slow.* 2011 (Anchor Canada)

Lebell, Sharon. *The Art of Living: The Classical Manual on Virtue, Happiness, and Effectiveness* (Substantially reproduces the main text of the book Epictetus). 1995 (HarperCollins)

Mitchell, Stephen. *Tao Te Ching* by Lao Tzu (Translation). (HarperPerennial, Modern Classics)

Newport, Cal. *Deep Work, Rules for Focused Success in a Distracted World.* 2016 (Grand Central Publishing)

Paul, Daniel N. *We Were Not The Savages: Collision between European and Native American Civilizations.* 2006 (Fernwood Publishing Company Ltd)

Pressfield, Steven. *The War of Art: Break Through the Blocks and Win Your Inner Creative Battles.* 2002 (Black Irish Entertainment LLC)

Rodskey, Eve. *Fair play: a game-changing solution for when you have too much to do (and more life to live).* 2019 (Putman)

Schwartz, Tony with Jean Gomes and Catherine McCarthy. *The Way We're Working Isn't Working.* 2010 (Free Press)

Sharma, Robin. *The 5 AM Club.* 2018 (HarperCollins Publishers Ltd.)

Sharma, Robin. *The Leader Who Had No Title.* 2010. (Free Press)

Sharma, Robin. *The Saint, the Surfer, and the CEO.* 2003 (Hay House, Inc.)

Tolle, Eckhart. *A New Earth: Awakening to Your Life's Purpose.* 2005 (A Plume Book, Penguin Group)

Tolle, Eckhart. *Stillness Speaks.* 2003 (Namaste Publishing)

Tolle, Eckhart. *The Power of Now: A Guide to Spiritual Enlightenment.* 1999 (Namaste Publishing)

Tsabary, Shefali. *The Conscious Parent: Transforming Ourselves, Empowering our Children.* 2010 (Namaste Publishing)

Acknowledgements

Thank you to all my family and friends who took the time to listen, review, and offer their much appreciated feedback.

I also want to thank those who were specifically involved in launching this project including Meg Ryan, Lee Thompson, and the wonderful Pottersfield Press team of Lesley Choyce, Julia Swan, Peggy Amirault, and Gail LeBlanc.

About the Author

Luc Desroches was born in Edmundston (Wolastoqey territory), and lived most his life in Moncton (Mi'gma'ki territory) where he studied and was called to the New Brunswick Bar Association as a lawyer, although not currently practising. Luc has been a Canadian federal public servant since 2004, presently working with the Impact Assessment Agency of Canada building and maintaining positive relationships with Indigenous communities.

Working from his home office since 2016 has allowed a more harmonious life with his beautiful wife, three daughters, and Labrador retriever. Luc is a strong advocate for teleworking by passionately writing and speaking about the subject. He also enjoys running, motorcycle rides, and spending quality time with family and friends.